Foreword by Nick Saban

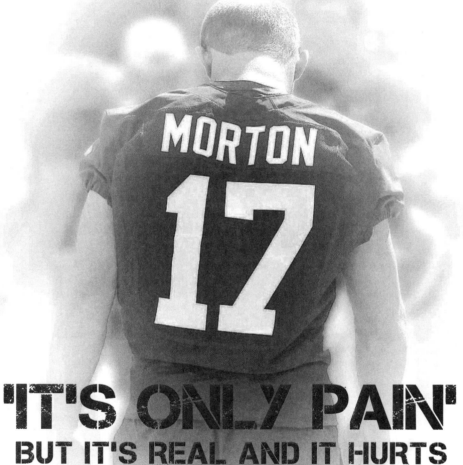

MORTON

17

'IT'S ONLY PAIN'
BUT IT'S REAL AND IT HURTS

By Taylor Morton
With Stephen Copeland

Published by The Core Media Group, Inc., P.O. Box 2037, Indian Trail, NC 28079.

Cover & Interior Design: Nadia Guy
Cover & Back Cover Images: Robert Sutton, The Tuscaloosa News

Printed in the United States of America.

*In loving memory of Trent McDaniel Morton
and David Gilchrist Karn.*

PRAISE FOR
'IT'S ONLY PAIN'

"I have known Taylor for several years and watched him develop into a leader capable of changing the world. Taylor has endured more than most young men in their twenties, but he has chosen to rise above and point people to Jesus when dealing with adversity. I hope his story will inspire and even equip thousands to respond much the same way!
-Brent Crowe, PhD, vice president of Student Leadership University

"Taylor Morton has faced things in his life that most people only experience in their worst dreams—moments that are game-changers and even game-enders. But Taylor's perseverance is an inspiration to a generation and proof that God can be trusted with the details of our lives. His book reminds me that Jesus didn't come to make good things better; He came to bring life out of death and hope out of hopelessness. You will be encouraged, challenged, and changed by his story."
-Acton Bowen, best-selling author and speaker

"Taylor Morton is a walking testament of the grace and grit of life. Taylor's captivating story is filled with tragedy one minute and triumph the next, both being used by God for His renown. I recommend this book wholeheartedly."
-David Nasser, author, speaker, and senior vice president of Liberty University

"I had the privilege of training hundreds of officers from around the world—teaching them to fly, fight, and win in the cockpit and in life.

I am honored to have Taylor as a close friend, to see him positively impact lives, and help get his story to the masses. Taylor's message will help you navigate life's storms, lead others safely through adversity, and stay in the fight."

-Lacy Gunnoe, "The Pilot Speaker," founder of Remove Before Flight, U.S. Air Force

"Rarely do you encounter the embodiment of tenacity, fortitude, and charisma mixed with humility, but the life journey of Taylor Morton is extraordinary to say the least. This book challenges what is at the core of every person—the necessity to persist and the passion to rise above all obstacles. Obstacles are opportunities that allow a story beyond oneself to be shared and expressed! Enjoy, read, glean, and seize the day!"

-Ed Newton, author and evangelist

"It's Only Pain is a powerfully inspirational story showing how God can take the trials in our lives and use them for His great purposes. As an athlete, I know the importance of struggles, for they create a consistent character, which in turn produces hope (Romans 5:3-4)—a great reminder to 'never, never quit!'"

-Kim Jacob, former University of Alabama gymnast and 2014 NCAA Woman of the Year nominee

"Taylor is a guy I wish I could be like. His drive for Christ and his hunger to reach out to people are gifts from God. We both have similar stories involving adversity in our childhoods. I wish I had the courage to stand up and lay down my life for Christ like he did. I look up to him more than anybody I know to this day. Taylor's story and testament not only inspires me every day but will also touch so many lives by just reading this piece he wrote."

-Ben Jones, starting offensive guard for the Houston Texans

"Taylor Morton is the real deal. In a time when we hear all of the negatives found in college athletics, Taylor's story is a breath of fresh air. *It's Only Pain: But it's Real and it Hurts* is a story of heartache, brokenness, and redemption. This is a must read for guys that are looking for more than just another football book. This is a road map for experiencing all that God has in store for you."

-Chuck Allen, senior pastor at Sugar Hill Church

"I had the privilege of coaching Taylor for three years at Bibb County High School, and I have never been around anyone as mature and solid in his faith as Taylor. Taylor's message is ultimately one of faith and hope. Taylor truly is an inspiration. Reading this book or spending time with him in person will change your life."

-Mike Battles, former head football coach at Bibb County High School

"Pain is uncomfortable so we desperately attempt to avoid it at all costs. Taylor has endured more pain than anyone should at such an early age. Rather than *react*, he teaches us how to *respond* to pain. His ability to rejoice in suffering has produced such endurance, character, and hope. His book will help you not only push through your pain, but be thankful for it."

-Jordan Kemper, founder of OneBody and international speaker for USANA Health Sciences

"Taylor has been a great example of perseverance since the day I met him—from battling through the incomprehensible adversities in his life to battling for a roster spot on a national championship football team at the University of Alabama. Every time I come across him, whether it is in a hospital or in a weight room or on the football field, Taylor remains upbeat and hopeful. In a life filled with adversity, Taylor's life proves that attitude, approach, and mindset are everything."

-Mark Hocke, director of strength and conditioning at the University of Georgia

"Taylor Morton has a message that will impact everyone. He has faced adversity both on the field and off like a champion. Taylor brings his best. That can be seen from the national championship rings on his fingers to the anointed words that spring from his mouth. Do not miss the opportunity to read this book. No one is immune from pain and suffering. However, this book will show you the strength to keep standing while walking through adversities in life."
-Scott Dawson, author, preacher, and founder of the Scott Dawson Evangelistic Association

"Every human will go through hard times. It's not a matter of 'if' but 'when.' And during those times we all need words of encouragement and hope. Taylor's book does just that. His life story of challenging circumstances—and his response—is a great testimony of perseverance and God's love. You won't be disappointed."
-James Spann, Alabama television meteorologist

TABLE OF CONTENTS

FOREWORD
BY NICK SABAN

University of Alabama head football coach

In life, and on a lesser scale in the game of football, the proudest moments and greatest victories occur when you see someone or a group of people come together to overcome adversity. Like we tell our players all the time, you are not defined by your circumstances; you are defined by how you respond to adversity and move forward. Taylor Morton has certainly set an example for all of us in how he responded to adversity and found a way to positively affect others.

Taylor was a member of our football team in Alabama from 2011 until 2013. We were fortunate enough to win back-to-back national championships in Taylor's first two years with us. Even though he wasn't as well-known as some of the players on those teams, he served in an important role as a walk-on defensive back and was one of the hardest-working guys we had on our scout team.

Guys like Taylor may not get the headlines, but they are the unsung heroes you need in order to have a successful program. I've said it takes a team full of champions to win a championship, and Taylor was certainly a champion on and off the field. Taylor is a fine young man who represented his family, the University of Alabama, and our football program in a first-class manner. It was a privilege to coach Taylor and get to know him while he was a member of our team. I have a great appreciation for the players who aren't given anything and who come here as walk-ons with the will to earn everything they get, especially those with challenges like Taylor had to face. More important than the wins or the rings he received as a football player, he is on track to earn his degree, and I'm very proud of him for that.

Taylor's story is one everyone should hear. It shows what perseverance and faith can do when life presents the greatest challenges. Taylor has taken the most adverse of situations and has worked each day to be a blessing to others. As you read, I know you will appreciate the message. We can all learn a lot from how Taylor responded to adversity.

FOREWORD
BY SCOTT COCHRAN
University of Alabama strength and conditioning coach

The energy on certain fall Saturdays in the University of Alabama's Bryant-Denny Stadium, when more than one hundred thousand fans roar as the young men wearing crimson and white run out of the tunnel behind Coach Nick Saban, is pure adrenaline. The Million Dollar band plays the fight song, and a sea of red shakers wave in a 360-degree panorama. The captains walk to the centerfield medallion, and with the toss of the referee's coin, the game begins. Sixty minutes, rough and tumble, hard licks, beautiful sailing passes: strategy, strength, and stamina. Bring it on!

But back up eight months to those days every January when young men line up in the training facility with talent, passion, desire, brains, and maybe a little ego, thinking that they can walk on to the team with eighty-five scholarship players and forty open slots to round out the roster. For the love of the game, maybe a family legacy, or maybe just to be part of a tradition of fifteen national football championships, they come. My job is to funnel this initial group of about one hundred or so down to the new players who will fill the open slots based on position need. Even if a player made the cut the year before, he goes through the same grind to prove that his strength and commitment to the team is fresh.

Coach Saban says, "There are two pains in life. There is the pain of discipline and the pain of disappointment. If you can handle the pain of discipline, you'll never have to deal with the pain of disappointment." My staff and I look for ability for sure, but beyond that, we look for dependability and a "buying in" to the discipline we expect.

Taylor Morton was that kind of player; he bought in and gave it all—weight training, learning the playbook, attending classes, keeping his grades up, and being ready to give 100 percent whenever he was called on to show up for the team. His exceptional attitude had that knocking-on-the-coach's-door enthusiasm that looks for advice and for ways to develop. Dependable, teachable, enthusiastic.

Taylor Morton is not just any young man. Through multiple setbacks, he has defined his life by helping others overcome adversity through faith in a loving, loyal God.

In my business, through training, goal setting, encouragement, and a little yelling, I push players to overcome obstacles and grow to their personal best. Taylor has chosen a motivational path that helps others meet the obstacles that blindside us in life, the tragic circumstances that arrive out of the blue.

He's been there. He knows the process.

He wants to help you build your faith muscles into the kind that can take the pain and move through it to higher ground, your personal best.

You got something for God? Bring it.

You scared? Read the book. Do the work.

1
April 1, 2007

"Given the choice between the experience of pain and nothing,
I would choose pain."
~William Faulkner, American writer and Nobel Prize laureate

I've been attending University of Alabama football games since I was five years old. Some of my fondest childhood memories come from Saturdays in Tuscaloosa when we would tailgate with our family friends, the Oakleys, in the morning; then play touch football at the Quad, the heart of the University of Alabama's campus; then head over to the Walk of Champions to catch a glimpse of all the players and coaches getting off the bus; and then sit right next to the Crimson Tide tunnel at Bryant-Denny Stadium during the game, where my family has had season tickets for years.

Each Saturday experience I had in Tuscaloosa growing up was unforgettable. When Nick Saban took over Alabama's football program in 2007 (I was in middle school at the time), I remember trying to get to the Walk of Champions ridiculously early just to catch a glimpse of him when the bus arrived. Then, when we took our seats before the game, I would sit there, anxiously awaiting my favorite player, Will Oakley (one of the Oakleys' relatives), to emerge from the tunnel in his crimson #7 Alabama jersey. I remember thinking to myself, *Maybe one day I could be like Will Oakley.*

I guess I grew up an Alabama fan primarily because of my father, Terry Morton. And my father is an Alabama fan because of an unlikely encounter with Bear Bryant when he was in grade school.

Stemming from a difficult childhood with an abusive stepfather, Dad began hanging out with the wrong crowd while in third grade at Stafford Elementary School in Tuscaloosa. Dad and his friends were once taken to the police station for recklessly causing fifteen hundred dollars worth of damage to a Tuscaloosa establishment.

When he stood before a judge in a Tuscaloosa courtroom and heard the judge say the words, "I'll pay the damage," Dad says he was humbled by receiving such grace, and his behavior was forever changed.

He cleaned up his act, and in fourth grade, his homeroom teacher nominated him for a citizenship award of sorts. In a single year, Dad says he "went from the 'Satanship Award' to the 'Citizenship Award.'" Because of his respectful behavior and exemplary grades, he and a half-dozen of his peers were granted the opportunity of a lifetime: a chance to meet Alabama head football coach Bear Bryant.

One day Coach Bryant visited Stafford and hung out with the selected kids. He talked to them about the importance of excelling in school and the value of friendship. They even got to eat lunch with him. Dad says he remembers Coach Bryant saying to them, "Listen to your mommas, and do what they tell you to do."

Later that day, he let each of the kids hold an Alabama game ball and said to them, "If you hold that football long enough, it will become a part of you."

Before Coach Bryant left, the kids got their picture taken with him, and it was featured on the front-page of the *Tuscaloosa News*. Dad still has the newspaper.

Ever since that day, my dad has loved the University of Alabama.

That Christmas, Grandma gave Dad a crimson #51 Alabama jersey.

When Dad was in fifth grade, Grandma and Dad moved to Centreville, Alabama, where Dad's grandparents (Grandma's parents) lived. Turns out, I'd be born and raised in Centreville; it's where my brothers and I would call "home."

Oddly, one of the main things Dad remembers from fifth grade involved two brothers in his class who were involved in a tragic hunting accident. (One of them accidentally shot and killed his brother.) This was Dad's first experience with tragedy and loss. For some reason, Dad says this has always haunted him.

Dad went on to graduate from Bibb County High School in Centreville and then Saint Bernard College in Cullman, Alabama. Upon graduating, Dad accepted a teaching job at Jemison High School, south of Birmingham. Soon after, he met my mother, Tammy. They got married and eventually planted their roots back in Centreville when Dad was offered a teaching job at Bibb County High School, his alma mater. He considered this his dream job. Mom got a teaching job, too—down the road at West Blocton Elementary School.

When my parents got married, they decided that they weren't going to have children for five years or so. Little did they know that having children would be more difficult than they ever imagined.

My mom had two miscarriages before I was born and a third miscarriage before my brother Trent was born. I was born on August 24, 1992; Trent was born on May 4, 1994; and our little brother, T.J., was born on May 18, 1998.

I'd imagine that three miscarriages in the process of having three children was a lot for my parents to handle, but I'm sure it was one of the reasons they were so thankful for us boys. As painstaking and heartbreaking as their journey might have been, I'm thankful they didn't give up on their dream of having children, because it led to my brothers and me.

Once I was born, my parents settled into a homey, one-story, three-bedroom house out in the country, right on the Centreville city limits. This is where they still live today.

Overall, Centreville seems to reflect the values my parents stand for—simplistic, down-to-earth, and loving. I would compare Centreville to Maycomb, Alabama, as it's presented in Harper Lee's classic novel *To Kill a Mockingbird*. It's a small, Southern town that is as intimate as they come. Centreville reported a population of 2,778 people in the 2010 census, and the county system only enrolls about 1,500 students from kindergarten through twelfth grade. Some high schools in Alabama have more students than our entire population.

To most, Centreville is just a Podunk town that is passed through, but for my family and me, it's home. People driving through Centreville on their commute to work or on their way to the mall or an athletic event often get held up by logging trucks on those small, two-lane, country roads.

The town's major employers, as in many small towns in America, are the hospital system and the school system. Small businesses—banks, grocers, eateries, cleaners, automotive services, hardware shops, and drug stores—line both sides of the Cahaba River that runs north and south through the town. Two bridges, the northern at Highway 82 toward Tuscaloosa and the southern at Walnut Street, connect the east and west sides of town. One of Centreville's fixtures is a two-story courthouse that is over one hundred years old; attached to the left side of the courthouse is a massive steeple that towers over Centreville's tiny downtown.

Needless to say, Centreville isn't a vacation spot, but my friends and I made the most of it growing up. We would tube or float down the river or go fishing in the many surrounding ponds.

What makes Centreville *really* special is the community. In Centreville, it isn't about what the town can do for the people but rather what the people can do for the town. It's strange to walk into a restaurant or shop and *not* know everyone inside. Growing up in Centreville is like having a 2,500-person family; you're surrounded by thousands of people who love you and deeply care about you. It was the perfect place to make memories and call home.

If you walked around in our home today, you might see some of those memories captured in pictures hanging on the walls of my father's den amidst a plethora of Alabama memorabilia—newspaper clippings, autographed footballs, and houndstooth Bear Bryant fedoras. They also adorn the mantle of our living room fireplace and are featured among the hundreds of relics in my father's office—swords, bullets, pieces of metal—that he has collected over the years.

One of the reasons my father loves relic hunting is that there is a story behind each item he finds. Who did the relic belong to? What was going on in the world at the time? What was the person, the owner of the item, struggling with? What adversity was the person trying to overcome? Of course, we'll never know. But Dad found it intriguing to think about—especially when a relic could be traced back in history to the Civil War or a specific battle.

Growing up, T.J., Trent, or I would sometimes go with Dad out into the quiet of the Alabama backwoods with his metal detector and shovel. Though I don't think we enjoyed it as much as Dad, it was still nice to be out there with him. Dad is the perfect father—the father he never had.

Today's, Dad's relic collection is scattered around his office, and a gigantic Betsy Ross American flag hangs on the wall. Later in life, Dad even took his collection, research, and findings and wrote a book about the Civil War. He hopes to get it published one day. On the first page of the book is a quote from William Faulkner: "Given the choice between the experience of pain and nothing, I would choose pain."

Dad says the quote not only summarizes history but also encapsulates his life—and mine as well.

Because Trent and I were only nineteen months apart—but one grade apart in school—he was my best friend growing up. We had the same friends, played on the same baseball teams, and were in the same Sunday school class.

I felt like our relationship and our adventures epitomized what it meant to be boys growing up in the country south—you know, like Huckleberry Finn and Tom Sawyer. Best friends. Always having fun.

One of our favorite things to do was go to my grandmother's house—which was twenty minutes away in Randolph, Alabama—and treat her property like a gigantic playground. This grandmother was my mom's mother, Wanda Fancher, and we simply called her "Nana." Sometimes, we'd go to Nana's for a weekend. Other times, on summer vacation for example, we'd stay for two straight weeks.

Going to Nana's was a blast. One thing I remember doing was setting up a slip-and-slide on the biggest hill on her property. We would lie out a plastic tarp and spray it down with soap and water. Looking back, it was probably extremely dangerous since the tarp was held down by a couple cinder blocks at the bottom of the hill. It was always a challenge to dodge the cinder blocks; if you didn't, you'd walk away with a busted face or skinned-up knees. This happened a couple times.

Overall, my parents raised Trent, T.J., and me to be active. Although we really enjoyed playing video games, we always felt like we were wasting our day if we didn't do something outside. Real adventures took place in *doing* something, preferably outdoors.

Of course, this included sports.

Athletics was at the center of our childhoods. Some might say, "Oh, football or baseball or basketball is just a game," but for my family, as for many Alabamans, sports were so much more than a game—they were a way of life. Sports were the way we bonded and how we had fun together. It was weird if we *didn't* have a ball game of some sort on a weekday evening or Saturday afternoon during the summer; it was weird if we *weren't* going to a high school football game on Friday night or an Alabama tailgate on a fall Saturday. It was rare for us to go to a movie or anything like that; there was hardly any time because of all the athletic events on our calendar.

The primary sport we participated in during those early years was Little League baseball. In Centreville, Little League was a really big deal, and it was often an all-day Saturday event. Again, this was particularly special for Trent and me since we were so close in age. I started playing when I was six years old, and Trent started playing when he was four. My parents actually got Trent started a year early just so he could be on my team. We played on the same team every other year all the way up through middle school. Trent always wore a #45 jersey, his favorite number.

Being able to play on the same team as Trent was not only convenient for my parents but was also a blast for both of us. As we grew older, our primary positions on the diamond were all too fitting—Trent was a pitcher, and I was a catcher. The dynamic between a pitcher and catcher can already be interesting, but when the person pitching to you is the person you share a room with, everything is heightened. I felt like I knew what pitch he was going to throw before he did. As we ventured through junior high, Trent was shaping up to be a pretty good pitcher.

I had hit my growth spurt a little earlier than Trent; I could actually grow a full beard in seventh or eighth grade, thus earning me the nickname "Man Child," whereas Trent had a baby face and was a little chunky. He was strong, though, and he had a mean fastball and a curveball with lots of movement. He didn't look that athletic, but he continued to grow throughout middle school and began to fill out nicely while we were still in Little League. Apparently my father never looked that athletic, either. He was only five foot eight in college but could still somehow successfully perform a tomahawk dunk. I wish I could go back in time and see something like that. Is there a relic for that? Anyway, Trent was beginning to take after my dad, turning out to be unassumingly athletic.

Our last middle school game together before I'd have to move to a different division in high school, I remember playing our cross-town rival West Blocton. Trent stepped onto the mound late in the game as a relief pitcher and got off to a rocky start. I remember pausing the game and running out onto the mound to talk to him. I don't think I gave him any advice; I just joked with him and tried to loosen him up a little.

He calmed down and ended up closing the game and getting us the win.

Following the completion of our middle school season, Trent transitioned directly into Little League baseball. Unfortunately, I was too old to play on his team. I hated no longer being able to play with him, but we both looked forward to the day when we would be reunited on the diamond in high school, when we could be pitcher and catcher once more, just as we had done for the previous seven years.

During Trent's Little League season-opener, he carded the best performance of his youthful career: pitching a no-hitter and going 4 for 4, all doubles.

Before the game, his assistant coach Heath Luvert had pulled Trent aside during warm-ups and said to him, "Play this game like it's your last."

Trent must have taken his advice to heart.

Growing up, the only thing more important than sports was our faith. It was family policy that we never missed a Sunday church service because of a sporting event. Although sports were a big priority in our family, nothing was more important than our relationship with the Lord. I remember Dad telling us, "Don't compromise the gospel of Jesus Christ for anything."

My family attended Centreville Baptist Church, across the street from the big courthouse on Court Square. Centreville Baptist looks like your typical, old-style church. It's built with reddish-tan brick and has six white pillars holding up a triangular overhang at the entrance of the church. A thin, white, pointed steeple climbing forty feet or so into the sky makes the church visible from just about anywhere in the downtown square.

Growing up, Centreville Baptist was as traditional as you might expect for a small-town Alabama church. Though the inside of the church had been somewhat modernized, wooden pews filled up the sanctuary and the balcony inside. The church service was just as old-fashioned as the building's outer appearance. No guitar. No drums. Just century-old hymns sung by a choir. (Today, church services at Centreville Baptist are not as traditional as they were in my childhood.)

Most Sunday mornings entailed Trent and me going to a Sunday school class taught by Wes Cash at ten o'clock in the morning, then going to "big church" in the sanctuary to sing hymns under the direction of music minister Mike Vickers, then sitting down to hear a sermon from Brother Ken Fuller, and then hanging out in the sanctuary after service for thirty minutes to an hour talking to just about everyone in attendance that morning.

After church, we'd usually go out to eat with our family friends, the Oakleys. We did everything with the Oakleys—from tailgating in Tuscaloosa to attending church together. Our family's stories have always been intertwined. Mike has been my father's best friend since fifth grade. Mike's wife, Sharon, is my mom's best friend. Like my family, the Oakleys also have three children: Anna Michael, who is my age; Trip, who was born a year after Trent; and Pate, who is T.J.'s age. After church, we usually found ourselves eating at Twix-n-Tween, a local barbecue joint. Twix-n-Tween was especially popular on Saturday afternoons in the fall, as people would come into Centreville off of US-82 on their way to Tuscaloosa for a Crimson Tide game.

If we didn't go out to eat with the Oakleys, Dad would sometimes take us to the Hit Pit, a nearby batting cage, or to the high school fields for an afternoon batting practice. If we weren't doing one of those two things after church, it was usually because someone had other plans.

Following Trent's Little League no-hitter on Saturday, I remember attending church the next morning and it being one of those Sundays when each of us had different plans after the church service. T.J. had a birthday party to attend—one of those weird reptile parties where you hold snakes and lizards. Trent went to our friend's house to fish, hunt, and ride four-wheelers. I attended a call-out meeting at the church for an upcoming mission trip called World Changers. Mom and Dad went home.

I was jealous that Trent got to go to our friend's house and have fun outdoors. Our friend was actually in my grade, and his family had fifty acres of property in the country, which included at least four ponds. We'd do everything out there—from fishing to hunting to four-wheeling to having airsoft gun wars.

The airsoft gun battles we had were always super intense. Although most of us had pistols, Trent had a sniper rifle and a machine gun. That's right, a sniper and an automatic weapon *that fired airsoft pellets*. No one wanted to mess with Trent during those battles. He took things to a whole new level. He even had a fake, plastic knife he would carry around with him. I guess it was so he could "go Rambo" on someone if things got real.

Later that day, Mom picked me up from church. I thought about heading to my friend's house to hang out with him and Trent but ended up just going home and hanging out with my parents for the remainder of the afternoon.

A little later, Dad left for his Sunday night deacons' meeting before evening service, and a half hour later or so, I started receiving a number of strange text messages.

"What's wrong with Trent?" the text read.

Not long after that, I got another text asking, "Is Trent in trouble?"

A few minutes later, another one: "Is Trent all right?"

My immediate thought was that Trent and his friend had gotten in trouble for some sort of mischief or something. A few more texts came in, and, as I talked to Mom at home, I decided not to mention anything to her. If everyone already knew that Trent had gotten into trouble, I figured she'd find out eventually. Nothing slips through the cracks in a small town; I figured she'd receive a call within the hour.

That's when we heard a knock on the door—I feared it might be a cop on our doorstep with Trent by his side. Instead, however, it was a family friend from church. It was a Sunday afternoon, so it wasn't uncommon for people from church to randomly drop by. Still, it was a little odd.

"Can I help you?" Mom said curiously.

"Oh, I just wanted to bring some chicken dinner plate tickets for

Taylor to sell," she responded. (At that time, I was selling boxed-up dinner plates to raise money so I could attend the World Changers mission trip later that summer.)

Mom welcomed her into our house, looked at me in the living room, and said, "Hey, will you take the trash out?"

"Sure," I said.

As I took the trashcans to the road, our friend's parents drove by. Again, this was nothing out of the ordinary; everyone lives relatively close to each other in a small town.

When they saw me, they stopped the car and lowered the window. "Your dad around by any chance?" the father asked me.

"Nah," I said. "Should be back soon. He's still at the church for a deacons' meeting."

"Okay, thanks," he replied, raising the window and driving off.

I went back inside.

No more than ten minutes later, Dad arrived back at the house. Oddly, Wes Cash, my Sunday school teacher, and Bryan Filgo, a fellow deacon, physically carried my father into the living room.

As they ventured closer, I noticed that my father had tears streaming down his face. I had never seen him cry before.

"What's wrong?" I asked him.

"Trent's dead," he said. "Trent's been killed."

2
'Never, Never Quit'

"Never quit. It is the easiest cop-out in the world."
~Bear Bryant, Alabama head football coach (1957–1983)

Everything stopped.

April 1, 2007.

The longest day of our lives.

Even now, it's difficult to recall what happened the rest of that day, nonetheless write about it. I do not know how to explain it, but it was as if everything began happening in slow motion.

Upon hearing the news, I remember my mother immediately leaving the room and breaking down. There were times I had seen her upset, but I had never seen her cry that hysterically and uncontrollably before. As I said earlier, having never seen my father cry, it was eerie to see both my parents in such a weak, broken state. Even when Grandma—the person who had adopted and raised Dad—had passed away three years prior, I don't recall him shedding a tear. If he did, I didn't see it.

Over the next couple hours, friends from church began showing up at our house. Before we knew it, there were over sixty people in our home, all tending to my father, mother, T.J., and me.

I don't think I cried that day, but that was probably because I was in shock and complete disbelief. Although everything around me seemed to be unfolding in slow motion, I felt like I was spinning internally. I just kept saying to myself, "No, this can't be real; this is not real; this can't be happening."

Any form of spinning eventually makes you sick. At one point, I remember feeling like I was going to throw up, so I went outside to get some fresh air. When I went outside, I saw my youth pastor, Scott Hunter, on the porch. "Man, I feel like I'm going to puke," I said.

I can't remember if I did.

Following the initial shock of finding out that Trent had died—and that it was true—the details surrounding his death were slowly revealed to us. The biggest question on everyone's mind was, "What happened?"

Apparently, Trent and our friend had been fishing and riding four-wheelers on his family's property—like we always did. Deciding to call it a day, they strapped on their helmets (his parents always required that we wear helmets while four-wheeling) and hopped on their four-wheelers to drive back to the house.

Getting back to the house entailed crossing a two-lane highway next to the property. In the spot where we usually crossed, there was a sharp, right bend in the road. Trent, driving in front of his friend, was crossing the street on his four-wheeler when a vehicle came around the turn and hit him, most likely killing him on impact.

We later heard that our friend, obviously shocked, hurried back to his house to seek his parents' help. When his mother and father arrived on the scene, his mother, a registered nurse, tried to perform CPR on Trent right in the middle of the street. She tried to do everything she could, but Trent was already dead.

I honestly still have a lot of unanswered questions about the accident. We have never spoken to the family who was in the vehicle that hit him. And to this day, I've never visited the spot of the accident.

Our house was flooded with family and friends throughout the duration of the evening. It wasn't until after midnight that they finally started to trickle out.

As I've said, I do not remember much about that day—it was a blur. I remember going out on the porch and feeling as if I was going to puke, and I also remember going back inside, seeing my mother bawling, and telling her, "It's okay, we'll see him again."

Saying this to her, however, only made her cry even more, and my dad gently told me that it wasn't a good time to say something like that. Now I know that it's vital for people to have the time and space to grieve.

For me, though, I immediately grappled for some sense of hope.

Even as an eighth grader, I looked for a solution. The thought of one day seeing Trent again was the only ounce of hope I could conjure up in my mind, so I clung to it. I recognize that trying to find something positive in the wake of losing my brother and best friend might sound strange, but it's how I've always reacted to things. It's not that I don't express emotion or that I didn't sink into sadness the day that Trent died, but I think most would agree that I express myself differently than others. Maybe one of the ways I grieve is by taking action. Plus, I was too shocked to cry.

That night, after everyone had left, Mom, Dad, T.J., and I all slept in my parents' bedroom. We did not want to leave one another. We needed that sense of togetherness.

We were all up early the next morning. It's difficult to sleep when peace is completely absent. As soon as we were up, people once again started showing up at our house.

It wasn't just our family that was grieving—the whole community was grieving. Our community had suffered loss before, but I cannot recall anything in my lifetime that was as serious and sudden as this.

In Trent's tragedy, there were no warning signs. It's not like he had an illness or even spent time in the hospital. In an instant, in a second, he was gone. No time for last words. No time to whisper a final "I love you." No time to tell him all the things I wish I would have said to him. Like a thief in the night, death swept him away.

We were a family most would consider "normal." We were involved in the local church, the community, and local education, with both Mom and Dad being teachers. All us boys, the Morton brothers, played sports and made decent grades. We were just a typical American family living in a small-town Southern community. In a single second, we were all thrown into the fire. The tragedy was one of those things where you couldn't help but say to yourself, "That wasn't supposed to happen to us."

What if Trent and our friend had caught *one* more fish? What if they had left the pond *one* second later? What if the vehicle had been traveling *slightly* slower? What if I had been there? Trent was hanging out with my friend, after all; looking back, it made no sense that I wasn't there with them. If I had been there, would it all be different? Would it have delayed things by one, life-saving second?

So many questions. So few answers.

Later on in the morning, I ended up going on a walk around the neighborhood with four of my friends—Anna Michael, Matthew Murphy, Justin Moore, and my cousin Jeremy Hobson. I think they were trying to help keep my mind off of things—you know, keep me distracted. It definitely helped. I don't know what I would have done if I would have been forced to sit alone in my thoughts and feelings.

When we got back to the house, Dad said to me, "Son, we need to go see Trent. This will be one of the last times you get to see him."

Honestly, I hadn't even considered this. In the chaos, seeing Trent hadn't even crossed my mind.

I didn't want to see his dead body, but I think Dad knew that I'd regret it in the future if I didn't go. I was scared to see someone who wasn't alive—that someone being my brother and best friend. Dad raised us boys to be fearless, especially in regard to athletics—no whining, no complaining, no victimization, no pointing fingers—but this, seeing a family member's lifeless body, was uncharted territory. I was terrified.

I got in the passenger seat of Dad's red 1991 Isuzu Trooper, and we left our house and made our way toward Rockco's Funeral Home, less than a mile down the road. I don't remember what Dad and I talked about on the way, but I remember trying not to think about what I was about to see.

When we arrived at the funeral home, we walked through the lobby and into an open room where they were preparing Trent's body. Trent was lying on a table, three or four feet above the ground, and there was a white sheet covering everything but his face. Two Centreville hairdressers who had cut our family's hair for years, Mrs. Tina Vining and Mrs. Sharon Deerman, were preparing his hair for the visitation and funeral. I noticed that they kept running their hands through Trent's hair and sobbing.

As I silently stood there, I'm not sure if I felt anything. It was an incomprehensible moment. Everything was numb. Trent had always been extremely active and vibrant, and for the first time, he wasn't talking, moving, or breathing. What was going on?

Unable to bare being there any longer, I took Trent's hand—cold to the touch—and held it; then I quickly left the funeral home and got back in Dad's truck. I sat down in the passenger seat and started crying.

Dad showed up at the truck soon after, and we silently drove home.

When we got back home, I felt the urge to go to my room, get down on my knees, and pray. Our house was still flooded with people, and some of my friends followed me to my room.

We closed the door, and I dropped to my knees. All the emotion that had been building within me over the last twenty-four hours burst from within me and came out as a prayer—a prayer of surrender.

"Here I am," I prayed as my friends put their hands on my back to support me. "Use me. I'm done going through the motions. I'm done playing this game called 'church.' The rest of my life, whatever I do, I want to bring glory to You. I want to impact others. I want to use this, I want to take this hurt, and I want to bless others with it."

Seeing Trent that morning, standing above him and holding his hand, had made me realize how little control I have in this life. It was the first time that the tragedy became real for me. It pulled me into unknown depths of pain, and simultaneously it made the hope of eternity more tangible than it had ever been. Though I couldn't explain the tragedy, the only comfort I received was from surrendering to Someone equally unexplainable, God, and hoping He had everything under control.

I understand this might all sound odd, but those who have lost a loved one might have felt something similar—a deep sense of sadness unlike any sadness ever felt before, mixed with a longing and hope of being able to see that person again one day. A character in Gilbert Morris's *House of Winslow* says, "Christians never say goodbye, son . . . Just until we meet again." I clung to this hope with everything I had in me.

Just as Trent's death became real to me for the first time, God also became real to me for the first time. As it's been said, you don't realize God is all you need until God is all you have.

On Monday night, we were given some of the things Trent had in his pocket when he died. This turned out to be a melted Snickers bar (Trent was kind of a chunky kid, so it didn't surprise me that he had a snack with him), a Ziploc bag of airsoft BBs, and a notecard.

This all might seem meaningless, but when you lose someone, everything that person owned suddenly becomes valuable. These material things are pieces of them, pathways into the life they lived, and opportunities to step into their world when you can no longer talk to or interact with them. All the little things become so much more important.

What was extremely fascinating was the notecard. When I first saw the card, I thought it was just a random piece of paper, as trivial as the Snickers bar and airsoft BBs. When I took a closer look at the card, however, I noticed it was a card that he had received from a ministry of some sort.

On the right side of the card was what looked like a runner standing on a medal stand in the pouring rain. To the left of the runner was text from Philippians 3:13–14: "Brothers, I do not consider that I have made it my own. But one thing I do: forgetting what lies behind and straining forward to what lies ahead, I press on toward the goal for the prize of the upward call of God in Christ Jesus."

In big, bolded yellow lettering above the Bible verses were three words: "Never, never quit."

To this day, I have no idea where he got the card or why it was in his pocket. All I know is that it spoke to me in a profound way. It was as if God knew that we needed something to help us press on and remember the prize amidst the incomprehensible tragedy we were enduring. It was as if the card was a love letter from God and Trent to us.

I took those three words and adopted them as my mantra. Despite all that I was feeling—despite the darkness that enveloped our family, friends, and community and that would continue to crash over us for years to come—I decided that I would not abandon my faith. I wouldn't quit on God. I wouldn't quit on my family. I wouldn't quit on my friends. I'd stay focused on the upward call of God in Christ Jesus—no matter what came my way.

In some ways, the card reiterated the prayer I had prayed in my room upon returning from the funeral home that morning. Pressing on and submitting to a greater calling—amidst the seemingly never-ending storm of pain and despair we were enduring—was a form of trust and surrender.

I asked my parents if I could keep the card, and I've held onto it ever since. Over the years, whether I was living at home through high school or in a dorm room or apartment in college, I would tape the card to the corner of my bathroom mirror, where I'd see it each and every morning.

3
Goodbye

"This is the end—but for me, the beginning of life."
~Dietrich Bonhoeffer, German theologian, pastor, and martyr

Whenever you lose someone you love, there's a weird feeling that, as bad as things may be in the moment, it's only going to get worse. It had only been two days—we hadn't even had Trent's visitation or the funeral—but it already felt like so much had happened. Those two days felt more like two years. When so many emotions crash over you, it's easy to feel like you are drowning. In order to cope, as I've mentioned, I became somewhat numb to it all. I was shocked.

The day before the visitation, my parents decided to set up a scholarship fund in memory of Trent—the Trent McDaniel Morton Scholarship Fund. My parents were quoted in the local newspaper saying that they didn't want flowers or gift cards but instead wanted anything of monetary value to be donated to the scholarship fund so it could have a lifelong impact on someone else. In the first two days, over $5,600 was donated to the fund. This was one of the first lessons I learned in the wake of the tragedy: to take our pain and use it for the good of others.

The following evening, we held Trent's visitation at Centreville Baptist. Nearly two thousand people, over half of the town's population, formed a line to pay their respects to Trent. The line circled the interior of the church and stretched a quarter mile or so down the road. It was as if nothing else in the world mattered but the situation we were going through.

The only time I looked at Trent was when we first arrived at the church as a family at five o'clock that evening, an hour before the visitation was scheduled to start. Mom, Dad, T.J., and I gathered around Trent and took a moment to marvel at the life that the person lying before us had lived. Trent was wearing his gray and purple, pin-striped middle school baseball uniform, and his face reflected a state of contentment and peace, as if heaven was as good as it was supposed to be. Today, his Little League uniform from his no-hitter is framed and hanging in our house.

For the remainder of the visitation, I made an effort not to look at Trent. It was too difficult. I kept my back turned to everything, as if unaware that my brother and best friend was merely feet away from me.

Though the visitation was only supposed to last from six o'clock to eight, it lasted from six to ten. For four-plus hours, Mom, Dad, T.J., and I sat on stools next to Trent as friends, family, and members of the community approached us and expressed their condolences. Life was an ensuing whirlwind, and the only thing I remember is asking Mike Oakley, my dad's best friend, to run to McDonald's and get me a double cheeseburger. I was starving and was emotionally and socially exhausted, and I felt like I was going to pass out. I know this might seem like a strange thing to remember, but when you experience something as tragic as the reality we were living, you naturally begin to block things out. Looking back, maybe I remember Mike Oakley bringing me food because it was one of the only normal, everyday conversations that I had that evening—and being hungry was such a normal thing to feel.

Once the visitation had finally ended, we all went back home. We didn't fall asleep until after midnight, and T.J. and I once again slept on the floor next to my parents' bed.

The next day was the most difficult: the funeral. For T.J. and me, it meant saying goodbye to a brother we loved; for my parents, a son.

Looking back, I cannot help but reflect upon the last time I had interacted with Trent—when he was alive, cheerful, and going about his life as a kid, just like me. I wasn't able to attend his no-hitter that previous Saturday, just a day before he died, because my parents had signed me up for a church conference through Centreville Baptist called Discipleship Now that was taking place that day.

Before leaving for the conference, I remember seeing him in our living room playing MLB Slugfest on our Xbox. He was wearing his baseball uniform, squeezing in a few minutes of videogames before leaving for his Little League game. We had some pretty heated battles playing MLB Slugfest. I usually played with the St. Louis Cardinals because of Albert Pujols, and Trent always played with the Boston Red Sox because of David Ortiz. What we enjoyed more than anything was intentionally hitting one another with a pitch and then having an old-fashioned baseball brawl. I always beat him in that game—although if he were alive today, he'd probably tell you something different.

Overall, it was just a normal day. I was doing something with church; he was doing something with sports—our family's two main priorities. I didn't tell him "I love you." I didn't tell him how much he meant to me. Why would I? Brothers at that age just don't stay stuff like that to one another out of the blue. But I wish I would have.

The funeral was at two o'clock in the afternoon. It was a Wednesday.

None of us were able to sleep, so we once again woke up early. We arrived at Centreville Baptist Church late morning. I wore a white shirt and black pants with a khaki sports coat and an Alabama Crimson Tide tie; there was a gigantic elephant on the tie.

Before the funeral, Nana had gone out and bought each of us nice suits for the funeral. We had some nice clothes already, but Nana wanted to make sure we had the best clothing for Trent's funeral.

Upon our arrival, we made our way to the basement—the old fellowship hall. The interesting thing about the basement of the church was that it happened to be the community storm shelter for the city of Centreville. The room was supposed to be a place where people could take cover during a storm and feel safe, but for us it was the exact opposite. There was no place to take cover. No place to hide or feel safe. We just had to deal with it.

We remained in the basement for quite some time, occasionally glancing up at the television monitors that were showing a feed from the sanctuary. Each time I looked at the monitor, more and more people had arrived and taken a seat. By half past one o'clock, there wasn't an empty seat in the sanctuary. People began gathering in the basement, the hallways, and some of the other rooms in the church. It wasn't long before people started lining up outside the church, just as they had done the evening before, to show their support for us. All in all, more than a thousand people were in attendance.

Looking back, I don't know how we could have made it through those three days following the tragedy without the support of the community. Whether it was showing up at our house the day of the fatal accident, cooking meals for our family in the weeks that followed, lining up for a mile outside Centreville Baptist for the visitation, or filling every space inside the church for the funeral, all our loved ones made one thing certain: we wouldn't venture through the storm alone. Though there's nothing that can fill the void for losing a brother—or in my parents' case, a son—thousands of people meeting you where you're at can definitely help. For us, it did.

At two o'clock, the funeral began. My family and I were escorted to the front row, where we took a seat in front of Trent. Once again, I tried not to look at Trent too much. It just didn't seem right. Everything that was happening seemed to stretch beyond the limitations of my mind and my heart, too. I didn't know how to feel or what to feel or how to express something that had so many emotions associated with it, emotions that left me shocked and paralyzed.

When we first walked in, I could hear people crying and sniffling. Never before had I been around so many people crying at once. I think one of the things that helped me hold it together was the fact that I was a little distracted because I was nervous about speaking at the end of the funeral. A couple days before, Miss Connie Hale, our former music minister, had asked if I had any interest in presenting the gospel and talking about Jesus at the end of the service. I said yes because I wanted to honor my brother. Still, I was nervous.

The funeral began with our pastor saying a couple things and then my youth pastor singing "Praise You in This Storm," written by Casting Crowns, which I had asked him to sing. My family's chief desire for the funeral was that people would be directed toward Christ in a time of suffering. In our sufferings we can strongly identify with Christ. Everything that was unfolding might have made us raise questions about God's plan for our lives, but we couldn't help but think about how lonely our suffering would be *without* God. As strange as it may sound, we wanted to use our platform—tragic as it may be—to reveal where the anchor in our lives is found, even in a storm. Our hope is in the Lord.

After "Praise You in This Storm," there was another speaker, then another song, and then it was Dad's and my turn to go to the podium and say a few words. It was comforting to have Dad next to me up there—I mean, as comforting as something can be in a situation like that. Like everything else that had transpired in the previous three days, I don't remember much about what Dad said or what I said. I just remember reading from a gospel tract that Miss Connie had given me and asking the congregation, "Does anyone here want to accept Jesus Christ as Lord and Savior?"

Fifty people or so stood up, and for a second, it felt like maybe something positive could come from the gaping hole in our lives that would never be filled. We clung to the hope that perhaps God could take a tragic situation and use it for good.

Following the funeral, at least a hundred people got in their cars and made the drive to the burial site—I now know that this is a lot of people for a burial. The single file line of vehicles stretched for a mile. I'm sure anyone who happened to be passing through Centreville had to have wondered what in the world was going on. Centreville's police chief even stopped traffic on Highway 82. It was as if the entire town shut down and tended to our family. Though the burial site was only a ten-minute drive away, it took thirty minutes or so to arrive at the site and get parked. Everyone just parked alongside the highway.

When I first got there, I spent a little time at the gravesite, but then I walked away, not wanting to see my brother lowered into the ground. I knew it was going to happen, but I didn't want it to happen—it was all so weird. So I walked away from the gravesite and entered a white, little church on the grounds. I sat down and prayed. Somehow, there was a transcending peace that was calming my soul. I cannot explain it, but I believed everything was going to be all right.

Upon leaving the church, I remember looking up into the sky and seeing a detailed cross in the clouds. To this day, it is the most supernatural thing I've ever seen or experienced. There's no way something like that happened on accident. I wasn't the only one who saw it, either—everyone there saw it. We were amazed. It was as if God was saying, "Trent is with Me; now his life begins; rejoice, everything is going to be okay."

It gave us all a tremendous amount of hope—that God was right there with us, that His presence would carry us through, that He had met us where we were and would continue to meet us where we were. All I could do was smile and say, "Thank you, God."

4
Empty Chair

"The death of a beloved is an amputation."
~C.S. Lewis, English novelist and lay theologian

"The work of restoration cannot begin until a problem is fully faced."
~Dan Allender, Christian therapist and author

"I thought I could describe a state; make a map of sorrow. Sorrow, however, turns out to be not a state but a process."
~C.S. Lewis

I want to mention that, in revisiting some of my past pain and darkest memories, I do not want to come across as being dramatic or rendering up a pity party of sorts. The last thing my family and I want is for people to feel sorry for us. Being a motivational speaker, it is actually very uncomfortable for me to dissect my emotions and all that Trent's tragedy entailed because I want to get to the "motivation part"—you know, the "hope part." In giving a motivational talk—say, to a group of businessmen—it's easy to graze the surface of suffering and then dive into concepts I hope will inspire them. In a book, it's a little more difficult to breeze through the emotion and grief the tragedy entailed.

At first, when I heard words like "emotion" or "grief," I was honestly kind of turned off. My family and I were hard-working, blue collar, country folk—not people who talked about our feelings or pain. I guess I always associated expression of pain with weakness. Growing up, I was taught to never whine or make excuses, especially in regard to athletics; I was supposed to pull myself up by my bootstraps and sport a smile along the way. Never complain. Never victimize. Ignore the pain and press on. Not long after Trent passed, for example, I fell on my wrist after my friend took my legs out from under me while I was attempting a layup during a pickup basketball game. My wrist hurt at the time, but I figured it wasn't anything serious, so I didn't say anything to anyone. A week later, I found out that my wrist had been pretty severely broken.

I share this story because brokenness and weakness are things most of us naturally try to ignore, myself included. Though discussing and acknowledging our brokenness and weaknesses can be an uncomfortable thing, I have learned that it is an important part of the grieving process—a necessary, crucial part of moving through trauma. Maybe this book is part of the process for me.

In the next few chapters, the manuscript will at times move slowly; however, I wrote this book with the hurting individual in mind, and I hope it will be an honest reflection of my personal journey through grief and an encouragement to those who are also going through that process. I pray you will see how valuable it can be to move through grief, even though my natural tendency was to "tough it out" and ignore the pain I was feeling. The reality is that pain is real and it hurts. And lastly, throughout all this, perhaps you will get to know the brother I deeply miss.

As time passed, everything faded back to normalcy. The meals that were cooked and delivered to our house became less and less frequent. Fewer and fewer people dropped by sporadically each ensuing day. Visiting Trent's grave went from a daily occurrence to a weekly occurrence to a monthly occurrence. Other tragedies, whether on a local, national or global scale, came and passed. The trauma we experienced was never forgotten, but it naturally became buried in the layers of soiled time.

The strangest thing about life fading back into normalcy is realizing how abnormal all the normal things are. My whole day, for example—from morning to evening—would be filled with reminders of Trent, especially as I went back to school and my parents returned to work. It was impossible *not* to think about the brother I had lost.

For example, say I saw one of our neighbors walking his or her dog in the morning before school—well, each time I saw a dog, I'd be reminded of Trent's dog, Sissy, his terrier that was hit by a car two months before his own death. Trent was a big animal lover, and he loved that little dog. Some of the last pictures taken of Trent were of him and Sissy. He was so upset when she got hit that Mom and Dad had to spend a lot of time comforting him and talking to him about death and what happens when you die. He put those pictures of him and Sissy all over his room as a reminder of the good times they had together. Now, months after Trent's passing, it was as if we were doing the same, and people were now comforting us just as we had comforted Trent.

When I got to school, the strange looks and awkward conversations were a reminder that things would never be the same. When you walk through the halls after something like that, everyone looks at you like you have a disease or something. No one knows what to say to you. Do they express their condolences? Do they act like nothing happened? Do they ask how you are doing? All this uncertainty results in not saying anything at all, so they just stare at you like you're an animal inside an exhibit at a zoo.

Of course, this wasn't their fault. We were in middle school, after all. How do you respond to a situation at that age? Most people want to help—they just don't know how. At the time, however, I was only a kid—at an impressionable age, at that—and it made me upset. I suddenly felt like I was different from everyone else. No longer relatable. I felt like I was on an island. Early on, I could tell that I was going to be forced to grow up much quicker than most. I could tell I was on a different path.

Participating in after-school activities, especially those that were sports-related, brought back some of the sharpest pains. Even casually shooting hoops and throwing the baseball with my friends weren't the same without Trent.

I vividly remember walking by the practice football field one day and seeing two brothers casually throwing the football back and forth. That was really hard, because that was how it was supposed to be, how it used to be—and also how it no longer was.

The fact that my eighth grade year was coming to a close made things even more trying. Up until the accident, I had been looking forward to entering high school the following year, because being in high school meant that I was one step closer to playing three consecutive years with Trent, whether that was sharing the football field with him on Friday evenings in the fall, or playing basketball with him in the winter, or catching for him on the baseball diamond in the spring.

Trent and I always dreamt about being in high school together, especially once I got too old to play in Little League. We longed to be on the field together again. My last middle school game on Trent's team (my eighth grade year, his seventh grade year), I remember telling him something along the lines of, "Well, I'll see you in high school, buddy."

We anxiously anticipated high school because we'd be doing what the Mortons did best: play sports with one another.

On the brink of finishing eighth grade, I had the sinking feeling that those years were now gone—before they had even started.

Something as simple as an after-school snack might even hit a deep spot within me. I'd be reminded of Trent's horrendous diet—how my parents had actually sent him to a nutritionist because all he ever wanted to eat were tacos smothered with cheese and ranch dressing or bread daubed with mayonnaise.

He would seriously order cheese-and-mayo sandwiches when we went to Subway—it was kind of embarrassing for all of us. He loved ranch dressing and mayonnaise to a fault.

These thoughts might have made me laugh on the inside, but they were also vivid enough to strike a deep, emotional chord.

Eating dinner as a family was, by far, the most uncomfortable. Growing up, my family had always made an effort to have dinner together just about every night. This sometimes became difficult with all the sports we played, but, much like attending church on Sunday, family dinner was a priority. We didn't sit around the television. We didn't eat in the living room. We didn't come and go throughout the evening, eating at our own pace. We all sat at the kitchen table and ate dinner as a family. No electronics. No phones. No distractions. This was "family time"—an opportunity to pray together, eat together, and talk to one another.

For some time after the tragedy, it seemed like there was always someone bringing something over for dinner and eating with us, or taking us out to eat, or inviting us over for dinner. But once everyone fell back into routine, we also fell back into ours. This meant eating family dinners again . . . around the same kitchen table, our plates on the same blue tablecloth, the same three baby photographs—of me, Trent, and T.J.—hanging next to the table on the dining room wall. But now there were four of us sitting around the kitchen table, not five. Four of us praying, not five. Four of us eating, not five. Not to mention, there were a lot more leftovers too, without Trent and his gigantic appetite.

I don't think anyone had the heart to get rid of Trent's chair, so it just remained there in the kitchen—four people and one empty chair.

The first time we went out to eat at a sit-down restaurant as a family following the accident, I remember the hostess kindly asking us, "How many will be in your party today?"

"Five," Mom responded out of habit. "I mean four," she corrected herself.

Mom always tried not to cry in front of us, but I remember her disappearing into the bathroom before we ordered our food.

When the sun went down, we'd be reminded of Trent's love for sunsets. Even when Trent was at a friend's house, he would often call my mom and say, "Have you seen the sunset? It's beautiful." Each time we saw a sunset following his passing, it was a reminder of the beauty that Trent found in life.

Trent was always drawn to the beauty of nature and the mystery of science. Every year, Mom and Dad would let Trent, T.J., and me pick one place where we wanted to go, and Trent would always pick the McWane Science Center in Birmingham. Nothing else. Trent always said that he wanted to be an astronaut.

The year before his accident, I remember sitting out in the front yard with Mom, Dad, T.J., and Trent beneath the stars as Trent asked awe-inspired questions and made inquisitive, scientific comments about the starry sky above.

As colorful as the sunset and as wondrous as the night sky, we knew that everything Trent is experiencing in heaven is far greater than any beauty this Earth has to offer.

Going to bed was another reminder that our "normal" had been flipped on its head. In the spring following the tragedy there was a depressing, sinking feeling when we went to bed that we'd once again be waking up to the same reminders about Trent the following morning—whether it was school, sports, family functions, or something as small as hearing a rap song on a television commercial (Trent loved hip-hop, especially TobyMac). There was always something.

Part of me liked these reminders of Trent—I didn't want to forget about him—but it can also be exhausting to be continually reminded of what you've lost.

As for T.J., I think nighttime was the worst. That's because not long before the accident, my parents had given me my own room, and T.J. had moved into Trent's room to share it with him. T.J. might have been young, but he had to have known something was missing after Trent's passing because he never wanted to sleep in his room after that; he slept in my parents' room or on the sofa in the living room or in my room.

In fact, for the next three or four years, hardly anyone even entered Trent's room. His room remained exactly how he had left it—disheveled bed sheets, clothes on the floor—as if it were a museum or something. Like the chair at the kitchen table, none of us knew what to do, so we just left his room as it was.

5
A New Day

"Jesus wept."
~John 11:35

"Death is not the end but is really a transition into the next life, the great part of life, that frees us up into receiving God's courage and his help."
~Max Lucado, Christian author

"Death is hell and night and cold, if it is not transformed by our faith. But that is just what is so marvelous, that we can transform death."
~Dietrich Bonhoeffer, German theologian, pastor, and martyr

The weird thing about trauma is that some of my experiences and memories before the accident seemed to blur—some of them just disappeared. Just as a child cannot remember time spent in the womb, I had a hard time recalling life's moments after experiencing something that dramatically changed my world. It was almost like being born again and starting life all over. And I wasn't the only one. Ever since Trent died, my father cannot remember many of his life experiences.

I can remember some things before Trent's passing, but those memories seem to come in pieces and fragments—none of them are very detailed, and I'm sure they come across as being somewhat vague. I picture it being almost like "shell shock" in a war zone. A bomb explodes, and though you might survive, your vision becomes unordinary and disoriented. You don't really know what's going on, and you're just, well, shocked—incapable of functioning normally until your senses click back into place.

That being said, as I attempt to describe my emotions during this time as clearly as I possibly can, I want to note that if some of what's to come sounds vague or scatterbrained, it's because my world was spinning and my vision was not always clear.

The spring of my eighth grade year was also a blur. Following the accident on April 1, another wave of sadness hit on May 4, Trent's birthday. Even today, springtime, as beautiful as it may be, comes with the hint of potential deception.

Later in my life, when I went to college, I remember my mom's co-worker telling her that she had been walking to Centreville Baptist one morning and noticed that some workers were planting some spring flowers nearby. She went on to tell my mom that whenever she sees these flowers in downtown Centreville in the spring, she is reminded of Trent. That's because she had noticed these exact same flowers while waiting in the quarter-mile-long line on the streets of downtown Centreville the night of Trent's visitation.

I say all this because this has become springtime to me: new life mixed with the memory of death.

Trent's birthday on May 4—our first without him—was hard, but at the same time, I think we were all still in so much shock that I'm not sure if it really hit us: a little rain doesn't seem like much after experiencing a hurricane. It was eerie nonetheless. He would've been thirteen.

There was, however, one glimmer of hope for me that came in the spring: football. Though I was finishing up my eighth grade year, all incoming freshman interested in playing high school football (which I was) were required to attend spring training at the high school.

Spring football turned out to be perfect timing. With everything swirling around our family—the accident, all the daily reminders, and Trent's birthday—football proved to be a healthy distraction for me. It was an opportunity to get lost in a game and express myself on the field—to take all the complicated things I was feeling and unleash the emotions that I didn't know how to express through athletics. Outside of sleep, football proved to be the only avenue in my life where I was *really* able to escape.

Not only did I realize football was an escape that spring; I also realized I was good at it. It's one thing to play well on the middle school team—it's quite another to be on the field with juniors and seniors and hold your own as an eighth grader. The coaches threw me out there and gave me the opportunity. I think I thrived on that, and their belief in me on the field seemed to also give me confidence and courage off the field.

In Bibb County's spring game against Calera, I remember playing middle linebacker and picking off their starting sophomore quarterback. I was so amped up when I intercepted the ball that I ran right up the middle, lowered my shoulder, and pummeled the quarterback, bulldozing right through the poor guy. After running over him, I burst into the open field and ran the ball back for a touchdown.

As I stepped into the end zone, I remember thinking of Trent and dedicating the touchdown to him in my mind. I like to think that Trent saw it, too.

Spring training came to a close, and I finished my eighth grade year.

The football coaches gave us a two-week break before summer workouts began, and I went on World Changers down to Tampa, Florida, the mission trip I mentioned earlier. Though the point of the trip was to assist the impoverished in Tampa, I felt like I benefited most. It was exactly what I needed.

Going to Tampa was a good opportunity to get away from Centreville for the first time since the tragedy. Though there's no way my family and I could have stayed afloat without our friends, family, and all the good people in our hometown, it also made it very difficult for me to escape, because I felt like everyone knew what was going on. It felt good to be around people in Tampa who knew nothing about me. To them, I wasn't the "boy who lost his brother"—I was just a kid. I really appreciated everyone's support in Centreville, but I admit that it felt good to be anonymous again down in Florida.

I think this ultimately gave me the space and isolation I needed to start processing the pain—to step out of my state of shock and enter the grieving process. The fact that it was my first church trip without Trent also seemed to thrust me to the forefront of dealing with loss.

We helped with projects around Tampa during the day, but at night we had worship services and listened to a message from a pastor named Eric Houseworth from McDonough, Georgia, who we all called "House." His message each evening seemed to hit me in my core. Despite all the questions that lacked answers about the passing of my brother, I couldn't ignore the fact that God was meeting me right where I was. It might sound strange to be overcome by the love of God at a time where some might question whether God is love, but that's exactly how I felt, each and every night.

I'm not a crier nor am I an emotional person. After all, I only cried once the week that Trent died, the worst week of our lives. But I seriously cried every night after hearing House's messages at the World Changers conference. This was weird for me, but I think it was my own form of grieving.

Ironically, the deeper I was pulled into the depths of pain, the deeper I was also pulled into God's love and grace, which I found to be sustaining. As the pain became more real, God also became more real. My hurts were met with tender care from the Creator, which made me trust God more. I knew that I would never be able to explain the events of April 1, 2007, but someway, somehow, I could explain that God loved me. It was as if I could feel Him picking me up and carrying me.

After a week of mourning and grieving at the World Changers conference, I wouldn't cry again for seven long years.

Though I felt encouraged at World Changers and had plenty of space to grieve, the grieving process was far from over. For me, grieving has been an ongoing thing. Even today. Since the void Trent left will never be filled, part of me believes that I might be grieving and processing his death until I, too, leave this earth. World Changers was indeed helpful, but the rest of the summer was still difficult. Right when I felt like I had dealt with one thing, doubts, questions, and insecurities about something else would abound.

I might not have ever slipped into a deep depression, as I know that many following a loss have experienced, but believe me, I had my fair share of dark days and moments. There were times I was angry at God—angry at Him for taking my brother, angry at Him for taking him before high school started, and angry at Him for making my family's existence so much different than most of my friends' families.

Even the little things would sometimes take my mind down a trail that left me lost and hopeless. I'd never catch another pitch from Trent again, and I'd never hit him with another pitch on MLB Slugfest. Then there were the big things. I'd never get to stand next to him on his wedding day, and I'd never get to hold his first child. These might not seem like the type of things you'd think about as a freshman in high school, but when you lose someone you love, the future can seem crystal clear—like it's tomorrow or something.

To be candid, I also found myself getting angry with the driver of the vehicle who was involved in Trent's accident on that fateful day. Actually, I don't know if it was the driver I was angry with or the lack of answers about the tragedy, which happened to involve the driver. How fast was the driver traveling? Was the driver distracted? Could the accident somehow have been prevented?

All of these things—these mysteries and suspicions—made forgiveness an ongoing battle and made the belief that "God was good" (as I had learned in church) even more difficult to accept as truth. Although I'm not sure if it was God's plan for Trent to die, it seems plausible to believe that God allowed it. And if He did indeed "allow" it, did this affect His "goodness"? I might not have been able to put these emotions or questions into words as a fourteen-year-old, but now that I'm further removed, it's easier to formulate some of the things I felt.

In my darkest moments, I would get mad at myself. The guilt I sometimes felt for not being there with him—on that day—could sometimes turn into anger and self-hatred.

"Why wasn't I there?" is a question I'll never be able to answer. Surely, my being there would have, at the very least, affected things by a second's time, right? I guess I'll never know.

Every day seemed to present a crossroads of sorts: I could either naturally drift into bitterness or I could consciously decide to get better. The latter took a lot more effort, but what's interesting is that I could almost feel God strengthening me in my weakness. Though I was naturally inclined to be angry, I couldn't help but wonder: What's the point of feeling like that all the time? Clinging to God was the only thing that brought any sense of peace—not a lot of peace, just enough to pull me through.

My parents wrestled with guilt as well. It's hard to say how many times each of us replayed the happenings—the ultra specifics—of April 1, 2007 over and over in our minds.

Most of Dad's guilt came from church that morning. . . .

After service had come to a close the morning of April 1, Trent had first asked Dad if he could go fishing at our friend's house; Dad had told him no. So Trent asked Mom if our friend could go fishing on our grandparents' property; Mom told him no as well.

Mom, however, felt bad that Trent was the only one of us brothers who wasn't doing something social after church. (T.J. was going to a birthday party, and I was staying for a meeting with some of the other youth in the church.) She didn't feel like it was fair to Trent to make him come home and have no brothers to play with. So she offered the idea to Dad that maybe they could let Trent go to our friend's house to fish. Dad changed his mind and agreed.

Dad says that he vividly remembers peering over the railing on the sanctuary stairwell to say something to Trent on the floor below.

"Trent," Dad said, "you can go. Y'all have fun. Be careful."

Trent smiled happily and replied, "Thank you, Daddy."

It's the last time Dad ever talked to Trent.

Dad struggled with guilt because he changed his mind. He wished he would have gone with his gut feeling and made Trent come home after church. Would it have changed anything?

Mom, on the other hand, struggled with the fact that there were three separate times that day in which she might have been able to alter the future.

The first was at church; she felt that if only she hadn't persuaded Dad to change his mind, things would be entirely different.

The second was later that afternoon when Trent called her to check in, and she asked him, "What time would you like me to pick you up? "

"What time sounds good to *you*?" Trent playfully said, hoping to stay at our friend's house as long as he possibly could.

Mom laughed and said, "You can stay there a while longer. I'll call you when I am about to come pick you up."

Hypothetically, I guess Mom felt like she could have picked him up sooner—and maybe this would have changed things.

The third opportunity was when Trent called her again a couple hours later and told Mom, "Miss T. [our friend's mom] said that she'll take me home tonight after dark."

"Okay," Mom replied, "that's fine."

Again, I guess Mom felt like she could have picked him up herself—and maybe this would have changed things.

Instead, that's the last conversation she ever had with Trent.

Like the guilt I felt for not being there with Trent, the string of events leading up to his accident—my Dad changing his mind, the opportunities Mom had to pick him up—resulted in a tremendous amount of guilt for my parents in the years that followed. Of course, none of them ever thought that something so horrific would unfold. But when life becomes unexplainably fragile, it's natural to start wondering what you could have done to prevent the tragedy from taking place. You begin to second-guess everything.

Just as God met me in my depths at the World Changers conference and continued to do so as I wrestled with guilt and despair that summer, it seemed as if He was doing the same thing with my parents.

One evening, my dad was feeling very down, so he decided to go for a jog on the country roads around our house in an attempt to get his mind off things.

While Dad was out running a mile or so from our house, a woman in her thirties pulled up next to him in her car.

"Coach," she said, lowering her window and driving up next to him.

Dad looked over at her quizzically, trying to figure out who she was.

"God wanted me to find you," she continued.

"What do ya mean?" he said, still unsure who she was.

"Do you remember me?"

"I'm sorry; I don't," Dad said politely.

"You taught me in junior high," she replied.

"Oh yeah," Dad replied, connecting the dots, beginning to recognize his former student. "I remember you. How did you know where I lived?" he asked curiously.

"I *didn't* know where you lived," she replied, "but when I got off work, I felt like God wanted me to find you, so I just started driving. He directed me this way."

Dad was stunned. "Why?" he asked.

"I wanted to tell you that my son was killed eighteen months ago," she said. "But God wanted you to know that your son is in heaven with my son. That's what God wanted me to tell you, that they're okay."

The cross in the sky at Trent's burial.

The messages that resonated with me each evening at World Changers.

The woman in the car who somehow found Dad running on a country road.

God undoubtedly showed up in supernatural ways in the pits of our suffering and despair. And He continued to do so—speaking through His people and through His Word.

One day that summer, a man named Joe Clark called our house. Mr. Joe, a cowboy who trained horses, was about twenty-five years older than my father; he was a man who was full of wisdom and compassion. He actually taught my parents' Sunday school class at Wilton Bible Baptist Church in Montevallo, Alabama, where I prayed to accept Christ when I was younger. There are few people who are more devout prayer warriors than Joe. He had a gigantic whiteboard hanging on a wall in his house where he would write down people's names and pray for each person on the board every day. Anything that Joe said was well respected because he seemed to be in tune with the very heartbeat of God.

My dad picked up the phone when Joe called.

"How are ya?" Joe asked, after identifying himself.

"I'm real bad, Joe," Dad admitted.

"Well, God put it on my heart to call you, Terry. There's a verse He wants me to tell you about."

"Please tell me," Dad said.

"What's the shortest verse in the Bible?" Joe probed.

"The shortest verse in the Bible is 'Jesus wept,'" Dad responded, pausing. "Why?"

"Do you know why Jesus wept?" Joe asked.

Joe proceeded to summarize the story of Lazarus—how Lazarus was ill and dying, how Christ allowed Lazarus to die instead of healing him, and how Jesus raised him from the dead four days after his burial. It isn't until John 11:35, when Jesus is in the process of raising Lazarus, where we read the verse, "Jesus wept."

"Yeah, that's what happened," Dad said matter-of-factly. "I don't get it."

Joe paused.

"Would you want God to bring Trent out of heaven now?" he asked.

"Well, selfishly, I would, but we don't know what he's experiencing in heaven," Dad responded.

"Maybe Jesus wept because Lazarus's soul was in heaven but was brought back to this fallen world. He had to bring Lazarus's soul out of heaven to be reunited with his body."

Joe Clark's phone call had a lasting impact on my parents because it comforted them to know that Trent's soul was in the best place it could possibly be—his truest home in heaven.

Earlier I mentioned that each of us felt an element of guilt about Trent's death, especially my parents, who viewed themselves as protectors and guardians of their children. Sometimes, I think this guilt seemed impossible for them to shake.

Joe, however, helped them with this as well. He once told them, "This has nothing to do with you guys; this was between God and Trent." I think it took a while for my parents to believe this, but maybe they began to believe it more and more over time.

Looking back, the events leading up to Trent's death were so improbable that it was as if he was destined to step into eternity that day. It was as if he was going to heaven that day no matter what variable was altered. Maybe Joe was right. Maybe this was about Trent and God, not anything that we had done wrong.

This was a freeing thing to believe. It was comforting to trust that God was calling Trent home—that maybe there was some truth in Job 14:5 ("Since his days are determined, and the number of his months is with You, and You have appointed his limits that he cannot pass"). This brought God's sovereignty to the forefront and therefore helped heal the guilt and shame we felt. Guilt over something you cannot control only leads to darkness, depression, and despair—and I know at times it did.

I still had a lot to figure out at a pivotal time in my adolescence, and I think God illuminated my mind with some practical, simplistic truths that helped me stick to the life-changing prayer that I prayed the day after Trent died.

For example, something deep within me knew that the trial of my brother's death would either make me or break me. I knew it was going to be a battle, and I was determined not to let the dark forces of negativity and victimization tear me apart. Author and speaker John Maxwell puts it this way: "You cannot always control what happens to you, but you can control what happens in you." Considering the Holy Spirit—the living God—lived in union with me, I figured this gave me a pretty good advantage in the ensuing internal battle.

I didn't want Satan to think for a second that he had an edge on me or even had the slightest chance of destroying me. The feelings of hate and sorrow were naturally going to come, but I believed I had a choice as to whether or not I allowed them to linger—to define me. I knew that losing Trent would either destroy my belief or deepen it. It would either destroy my life or help me live with more meaning and purpose because I had a unique understanding of how frail life was.

One thing that helped me throughout the grieving process was realizing that life is a gift—and therefore, Trent's life was a gift. Something that makes life so special is death. If we never died, life wouldn't be all that important. On a similar note, I recently encountered one of the most elegant writings on death I've ever read—by pastor and theologian Dietrich Bonhoeffer, who died for the cause of Christ in a concentration camp in Nazi Germany. Bonhoeffer writes:

That life only really begins when it ends here on earth, that all that is here is only the prologue before the curtain goes up—that is for young and old alike to think about. Why are we so afraid when we think about death? Death is only dreadful for those who live in dread and fear of it. Death is not wild and terrible, if only we can be still and hold fast to God's Word. Death is not bitter, if we have not become bitter ourselves. Death is grace, the greatest gift of grace that God gives to people who believe in him. Death is mild, death is sweet and gentle; it beckons to us with heavenly power, if only we realize that it is the gateway to our homeland, the tabernacle of joy, the everlasting kingdom of peace.

How do we know that dying is so dreadful? Who knows whether, in our human fear and anguish we are only shivering and shuddering at the most glorious, heavenly, blessed event in the world? Death is hell and night and cold, if it is not transformed by our faith. But that is just what is so marvelous, that we can transform death.

Viewing Trent's life as a gift from God and understanding death as grace allowed me (and still allows me) to approach everything about Trent's life as a blessing from God: the twelve beautiful years we spent together, the late-night talks in our bunk beds, the pitcher/catcher conversations we had on the mound during a game, the football games and the church retreats, the summers at Nana's and the family vacations, the long days we spent fishing at the pond or playing "war" in the woods—I could go on and on.

Of course, reflecting on these things makes me miss him even more and still causes some feelings of sadness and despair to well up within me, but the reality is that I would rather have shared these moments with him than *not* shared these moments with him. His life was a blessing to me, our family and friends, and thousands of others. Though his time on earth might have been shorter than most, all our lives are better for having experienced who Trent McDaniel Morton was.

And who exactly *was* Trent Morton? He was God's child—his belonging to God was at the very core of his identity. Before he was my parents' son or our brother, Trent was God's child. Just like William Faulkner's quote a few chapters before says, if my parents had to choose between grief or nothing, they would choose grief; as trying as the grieving process was, twelve years with Trent was better than a life without Trent.

My tendency was to pray self-centered prayers and ask victimizing questions:

- Why would You take *my* brother?
- Why would this happen to *me*?
- Why would You put *me* through this?

And, whereas I think that God appreciates the transparency and raw emotion in those prayers, what brought me the most peace was realizing that Trent did not belong to me or us. Trent belonged to God, and his life was a blessing *from* God *for* all of us. I think our tendency, whether we've lost someone or not, is to adopt a sense of entitlement in our lives. But realizing that everything in this life is a gift from God seemed to flip my me-centered world on its head.

I have learned that journeying through the thick mud of grief—and everything it entails—can be a positive and beneficial thing. As messy as the journey may be, it's an opportunity to discover who you are, who God is, and who you are in Christ. I think the gospel itself reveals that transcending hope and joy is most vividly demonstrated in the depths of suffering. Jesus, after all, suffered an excruciating death before the triumph of the resurrection.

During this time of grieving heading into my freshman year, I remember dwelling on Romans 8:28: "And we know that in all things God works for the good of those who love him, who have been called according to his purpose." Now, "God has a plan" might be one of the worst things for someone who is suffering to hear, but for me, this verse took things further; it reminded me that God *can* work everything, absolutely everything, in my life for good, no matter how dark or hopeless a situation might seem.

God had already graciously brought Trent into our lives, blessed all of us with his life, and He would therefore make something good of the life Trent had lived. Rather than exhausting myself trying to answer the "Why?" questions of life, this verse helped me anticipate and look forward to how God might answer the "How?" questions of life: How would God turn this horrible situation into something good? How would God use Trent's life and his death to bless others? Those questions were yet to be answered, but they brought me the hope that I needed to keep pressing on.

It was therapeutic for me to place my hope in the mystery that God could make something positive of all the pain we were experiencing. And, though I knew there would always be a hole in my life that would never be able to be filled, I tried to rest in the hope that there might be some sort of meaning or joy on the other side (and in the midst) of our sufferings.

This was met with a conscious decision to begin a new day—and to begin a new day again and again for as long as it took. The circumstances my family had to deal with in Trent's passing were not easy, but I liked to believe that there was Someone who was even greater than my circumstance: God. I wasn't made to wallow in my self-pity or sulk in my sorrows for the rest of my life, because the Spirit of the Living God within me was a lot stronger than my circumstances. If I was forced to deal with Trent's passing alone, I probably would have wound up being a bitter and angry soul who despised God, but I didn't deal with it alone. God was there for me, embracing me and meeting me where I was.

It might take a few days of starting a new day. Maybe a few years. Or maybe a lifetime. But as I entered my freshman year, I figured it was up to me to make that choice, each and every day—to take little steps toward hope, to choose positivity over negativity, to believe I was a blessed child of God rather than a victim.

I might not have had a choice when it came to losing my brother, but I had a choice to start a new day, a choice to believe that I could begin again . . . and again . . . and again.

6
Touchdowns and Angels

"We are products of our past, but we don't have to be
prisoners of it."
~Rick Warren, author of *The Purpose-Driven Life*

Though entering high school that fall brought the eerie feeling that I'd never get to enjoy that particular phase of my life with Trent, I continued finding a positive avenue of escape in football.

Every day, I looked forward to getting out on the field for practice and getting lost in the most beautiful game ever created. Whereas so much of my life felt like I was breathing out, football seemed to breathe into me.

This is the effect football seems to have on most people in central Alabama.

They say football is a religion in Alabama, and if you ever dropped by Bibb County High School on a Friday evening in the fall for a home football game, you'd understand why. Cheering on the purple and gold Bibb County Choctaws (named after Native Americans originally from the Southeastern United States) was *the* thing to do and still is today. Home games in Centreville are treated like a holiday. The town shuts down—for a couple hours, at least—and seemingly everyone comes together as one. People would come out of the woodwork to watch some Bibb County football. The game itself offers a one-of-a-kind atmosphere, and after a victory, things can get pretty rowdy.

Growing up, some of my fondest memories come from cheering on the Choctaws on Friday evenings beneath the lights. In fact, that was the only good thing about summer vacation ending and returning to school—it meant football season was beginning. Those Friday night games seemed to kick off a weekend of football for the Morton family. Choctaws on Friday night. Crimson Tide tailgate on Saturday morning before the game in the afternoon.

During those Choctaw games in my youth, Trent and I would usually play tackle football with our friends in the practice field behind the end zone.

Sitting in the stands at the Bibb County games as a child gave me a sense of wonder and awe for the players on the field, as if they were gods. The Choctaw chants. The sea of purple. The sights. The smells. The feeling of victory and the joy it brought to the town. It was much more than just a football game—it was something the community did together, as one.

As a kid, I wondered if that would ever be me one day, if I'd ever be good enough to have a crowd watching me. I didn't know if I ever would, but in the blink of an eye, as my freshman season rapidly approached, that day finally came.

On top of Alabamans' natural obsession with football and Centrevillians' general passion for football, there was also a lot of hype around our team my freshman year. That's because we were loaded with talent.

We had junior running back Zac Stacy, who went on to play college football at Vanderbilt University and was later drafted by the St. Louis Rams in the 2013 NFL Draft. And we had senior lineman Ben Jones, standing at six foot three and weighing 250 pounds, paving the way for Zac. Ben went on to play college football at the University of Georgia and was drafted by the Houston Texans in the 2012 NFL Draft. Their skill sets combined gave us one of the most dangerous rushing offenses in the state.

Growing up, Ben always felt like an older brother to Trent and me. My parents remember Ben volunteering at Centreville Baptist when we were in grade school and helping Trent make an LSU logo with those fusible beads that you iron together. They were probably supposed to make crosses or something religious since it was at church, but Trent loved the logo, and my parents still have it.

Ben and I also related well because we had both lost a family member. Ben's dad had passed away when he was younger, so after Trent's passing, I confided in Ben a little about how I struggled with loss because I knew he could relate. He was a heck of a player on the field, but what he did for me off the field is something I'll forever be grateful for.

The varsity coaching staff proved to be an outlet for me as well. Bibb County's head football coach my freshman year was a kind, intelligent man named Darryl Burns. Coach Burns was a strong Christian who was entering his first year as Bibb's head coach. He and his staff were encouraging and supportive of me in my unique situation. They didn't coddle me, but they were approachable, and I felt comfortable talking to them about things if I needed to.

Apparently they believed in me on the field, too, because they told me I would be starting the first game of the season on both sides of the ball—linebacker on defense and backup fullback on offense. Heading into the regular season, I figured I would see plenty of time on the field. For a freshman in high school, that was pretty cool.

The day before our first game of the season, the LSU Tigers, Trent's favorite team, played their season-opener against Mississippi State. With it being the first LSU game since Trent's passing, we watched the game together as a family at our house in Centreville.

We have no idea why Trent loved LSU so much, but Dad remembers Trent saying, "I'm gonna root for someone other than Alabama." (I think Trent said this because he wanted to root for a different team than the rest of us—middle-child rebellion perhaps.)

"That's fine," Dad told him, "but I can't let you root for the Auburn Tigers." That would have been sacrilege in our house.

"Hmmm, Tigers," Trent said. "How about the LSU Tigers?"

"Yeah, I'm with that," Dad said.

No one excommunicated him from the family for liking LSU. But had he chosen Auburn, it might have been a different story.

Trent was unashamed of his love for LSU, even in our Alabama-and-Auburn saturated area. He had LSU clothing, banners, and posters hanging in his room, and he watched every game. Sometimes Trent wouldn't even come to the Alabama tailgates and games with us because he wanted to stay home or go to his best friend Kendal Hubbard's house to watch his Tigers. Kendal pulled for LSU because Trent, his friend, pulled for LSU.

When people thought of Trent, one of the first things that came to their minds was his love for LSU. Just one season before, Trent and Dad had gone to an LSU/Alabama game at Tiger Stadium, Trent's first time in Baton Rouge. Since his passing, Nana had even stitched a big, comfy, purple-and-gold LSU blanket for our family. If you visited my parents' house today, you would most likely see it stacked upon a pile of blankets next to our sofa.

It was sobering to watch the Tigers play that Thursday evening, thinking about how excited Trent would have been for another LSU football season, especially considering they were entering the year ranked No. 2 in the country. It was LSU's year to win it all. If Trent were alive, he most likely would have been in the living room with us, sitting cross-legged in front of the television with his eyes glued to the screen and wearing his #4 LSU JaMarcus Russell jersey.

In short, watching the game was another vivid reminder of the void we felt; yet, being in touch with the pain was the only way to feel closer to Trent. It was paradoxical.

As for the game, it was never close. The Tigers picked off six throws and ran away with the victory. However, the most shocking thing about the evening was the score of the game. LSU defeated Mississippi State 45-0.

Forty-five.

Trent's favorite number.

The number he always wore in Little League.

Of all the points LSU could have scored in their victory, they scored forty-five.

Was it just a coincidence, or was God at work?

We were all overcome, and we sat there in silence after LSU's victory, chills running up our arms and legs. It was as if God was once more reminding us of His presence, once more meeting us in our emptiness, once more reminding us of the life Trent lived—and helping us feel close to our beloved family member.

Our first game of the season was the day after the LSU game, August 31, 2007. It was an away game against Greensboro East High School, which was about forty-five minutes away. Being my first competitive game since Trent's passing, and considering what we had experienced the night before, my emotions were running high. I'll always remember putting on my purple-and-gold Bibb County Choctaw jersey in the locker room, standing in front of the mirror, and thinking to myself, "Trent, this is for you."

I also started a tradition that I continued for the remainder of my high school career. I taped my wrists and wrote "Trent 45" on one wrist and "Never Quit" on the other. Not only was football an escape for me, but it also felt like an opportunity to connect with my brother. Everyone else was playing a game. But I felt like I was playing a game for him.

After winning our first game of the season 49–8 over Greensboro, we geared up for our home opener the following week against Shelby County.

Taking the field for the first time in front of a packed home crowd was unforgettable. It was like stepping into a bank of memories. I might have only been a freshman, but it felt exactly right to be there in that place.

What added an interesting dynamic for me on a personal level was the fact that I was playing in front of a thousand people who knew my story. Imagine playing in front of that many people who all knew the darkest moment of your life. And, whereas this was somewhat of a strange feeling for a fourteen-year-old kid, it was also extremely uplifting to feel everyone's support. Everyone wanted to see me excel out there because they knew what my family had been through. They could see the story I was carrying.

Midway through our home opener, I took a handoff, received a good block from Ben Jones (every block of his seemed to be a good block), and ran up the middle. A hole opened up, as if it was the Red Sea parting, and I exploded past the opposing defensive backs and safeties—ten, twenty, thirty, forty, fifty-five yards for a touchdown. Though I might have struggled to express myself vocally after the tragedy, I had no problem expressing myself on the field.

As I ran into the end zone, I felt like I was living in a movie.

I don't even remember my teammates' reaction or the crowd's reaction after my touchdown—it was as if everything went silent. It was a moment between God and me—a time not only to run into the end zone but also to run into His arms, to rest in Him. I pointed toward the heavens and thanked God for the moment.

"I wish you could see it," I said under my breath.

I like to think Trent did.

7

When Christmas Never Came

"In some ways suffering ceases to be suffering at the moment it finds a meaning, such as the meaning of a sacrifice."
~Viktor Frankl, neurologist/psychologist and
Austrian Holocaust survivor

We won the first five games of my freshman season and lost our last five out of six. I scored a couple more touchdowns throughout the year and continued to play on both sides of the ball as a fullback, linebacker, and defensive end. Despite the lackluster finish to our season, the year was a step in the right direction—we advanced to the 5A playoffs for the first time in several years, and we made a lot of improvements throughout the year.

In Alabama, there are six classes of high school football: 1A through 6A (as of 2015, it is 1A through 7A). Teams made the playoffs depending on how they performed in their individual regions. We had six teams in our region, and the top four made the playoffs. From there, all the playoff teams are seeded, and there are four single-elimination playoff rounds en route to the state championship game, which is played at Bryant-Denny Stadium, Alabama's home field, or Jordan-Hare Stadium, Auburn's home field. It's funny that the Alabama/Auburn rivalry is even woven into the state's high school football playoff system. There's not a chance in the world Alabama or Auburn would let each other host the state championship game every year—it's too good of a recruiting opportunity. So they rotate.

There'd be no talk of the state championship my freshman season, however. Our 2007–08 season ended with a 27–7 loss to Williamson in the first round of the playoffs. That game, for some reason, I remember hearing some of the opposing coaches yelling things from the sideline like, "Keep an eye on #22, the freshman white boy! He's fast!" I only say this because word seemed to be getting out that I could play—or could run, at least.

Overall, my freshman season of football not only provided me with a healthy outlet during a period of loneliness and helped me "step out of the fog," if you will; it also provided me with a lot of confidence moving forward. Sometimes when you experience trauma or loss, the simplest forms of positivity can have long-lasting impact on your well-being, giving you a taste of life again. For anyone venturing through the valley of suffering, I recommend finding a healthy, positive avenue of meaning—whether it's playing a sport or working on a difficult project or volunteering somewhere or getting plugged into an encouraging community.

I experienced this type of meaning through a game called football.

All the opportunities the coaches gave me and all my positive feelings associated with playing football only fueled my desire to get better. Now that I could see more clearly that I had been given a talent, I wanted to use that talent to the best of my ability. That meant nurturing and developing the talent, protecting it, and doing everything I could to help it grow. During the season, that meant training with the mindset that I was going to work harder than everyone else and walking off the field with the confidence that I had improved. In the offseason, that entailed being the first in the weight room and the last to leave. When it came to the games, I wanted to have an edge on my opponent solely because of my work ethic. I couldn't control whether or not I was as talented, but I could control how hard I worked.

On the mental and spiritual side, football allowed me to feel some sense of joy and excitement again, emotions I hadn't felt since before Trent's passing. God seemed to be using a little game with a pigskin as a way of helping me experience freedom and tranquility. When I mentioned earlier that football seemed to be breathing into me, these were some of the positive experiences I was referring to.

I was also beginning to realize that my story and the way I reacted to my story had the ability to impact people and point them toward something bigger. Football was a way to relate to people, and my story, depending on how God used it, had the potential to impact them. You don't really think about that stuff in junior high—those years are mostly fun and games—and maybe you don't think about it much in high school, but I had been forced to grow up quickly.

This was one of the ways I adapted in the wake of losing my brother: I discovered something deeper and invested in something I found meaningful. Everything became spiritual. A touchdown, for example, became so much more than a touchdown. It became an opportunity to praise God for His blessings in a time of suffering, a chance for my actions to reflect the story He was authoring.

The first semester of my freshman year was somewhat of a turning point for me because of all the positive things I experienced through football. Returning to my previous metaphor, the "shell shock" seemed to be wearing off—I was less disoriented—and I was beginning to see things clearly again. I was able to experience real joy and meaning for maybe the first time in my life.

The only negative about seeing things clearly again, however, is that you also begin to see all the damage that has been done. As the smoke clears and your senses straighten, you also notice all the debris and wreckage. Although it was difficult for us to register Trent's first birthday without him because it was only a month after the tragedy, the reality that he was no longer with us really began to sink in as Thanksgiving and Christmas approached. Around that time, I think my mother and father entered their lowest state on the spectrum of grief.

Mom and Dad tried not to cry around T.J. and me during that time because they didn't want us to think that we were any less important than Trent. They didn't want us to think that they were giving up on our family since Trent was gone. They wanted us to know that we were still deeply loved and that the most important thing to them was their children, even if one of them had tragically passed away.

One day, however, I remember Mom being unable to hide her emotions. T.J., who was only nine years old, noticed Mom was feeling down and asked her, "What's the matter, Momma?"

"Well," she told him, "I'm just sad about Trent."

T.J. then looked at Mom and said, "But Momma, Trent is in heaven."

The reason I share this story is because it shows the simplicity of the childlike faith that Jesus talks about in the Bible. I think it also shows how difficult it was for my parents on a daily basis not to slide into an all-consuming depression that would certainly affect their parenting.

One thing that helped my mom was finding a safe place where she could express herself and feel understood. One of these places was The Compassionate Friends of Tuscaloosa, a support group dedicated to helping parents cope with the death of a child. She was hesitant to attend at first, but she immediately felt comfortable in the group when the first thing the founder said to her was, "Tell me about Trent." Whereas so many people felt awkward or uncomfortable whenever my mom talked about Trent, The Compassionate Friends seemed to understand that Trent was the exact subject that Mom needed to talk about the most.

Mom said that having this outlet of sharing with other people who were wrestling with similar struggles and unexplainable emotions helped her remain a reliable parent to T.J. and me, despite all the crippling things she might have been feeling. This group freed her up emotionally and inspired her to further dive into her parenting. Just as I found meaning in honing my skills as a football player, Mom ultimately found a lot of meaning in focusing on her family: us. She's told a number of people that if it weren't for T.J. and me, she's not sure how she would have been able to go on with life. Focusing on being a mother helped her fill the void of no longer being able to be a mother to Trent. She often told herself, "Get up and go, or lie down and die." To her, getting up and going meant diving into being a mother.

As for Dad, his coping mechanisms were more comparable to mine. Dad is a lot like me in the sense that he really enjoys the challenge of working toward a goal or helping people through something that is fun and enjoyable. Dad is happiest when he's doing something or working on something. We both find joy in hard work. For me, this was through football. For him, it would end up being basketball.

The fall of my freshman year, Dad became Bibb County High School's head basketball coach. He had been offered the job several years before, but the time wasn't right; then, less than a year after losing Trent, the coaching position resurfaced. I think it was a handcrafted opportunity by God during a time when Dad needed it most. Instead of rotting thinking of all that he had lost, Dad had the chance to invest in something else. After watching each and every one of my football games in the fall, he was able to dive into another sport in the winter: basketball. Having spent much of his childhood and young-adult life playing basketball, I think he really enjoyed being around the sport again.

I tried out for the varsity team and made the squad, too. Dad was a great coach. The basketball team had only won five games or so the previous season, but Dad led them to a 13–14 record his first season at the helm.

As for T.J., though he might not have fully understood all that was going on, I think the saddest thing for him was the fact that he didn't get to experience the simple joys of having a childhood. He was thrown into the fire, just like all of us, and was forced to cope, just like all of us.

As the Alabama months grew cooler and as the holidays drew nearer, we were confronted with the reality that Trent would not be with us at Thanksgiving or Christmas. This knocked us off our feet.

Every Thanksgiving, our immediate and extended family would all gather at Nana's house for dinner. Dad was always the one who blessed the food, and this particular Thanksgiving, I remember him praying, "Thank You for this family that we have with us, and thank You for the years we had with Trent."

We had a tradition every Christmas Eve, too. We would go to Nana's, and she would read the Christmas story to us from the Bible.

As a little kid, listening to the Christmas story felt like it took an hour. All we (T.J., Trent, my cousin Kirsten, and I) could think about as Nana read from the second chapter of Luke was the one present each that we were allowed to open afterward. That was the rule: *We could open one present on Christmas Eve and the rest on Christmas Day.*

However, each year, the present that Nana gave us on Christmas Eve was a pair of pajamas. I'm not sure why we always thought it might end up being something different. To this day, I always leave Nana's on Christmas Eve with a pair of pajamas.

The best present I ever received was on Christmas Day 2003. If Trent were alive today, I think he'd agree it was the best present he received, too.

Boxing gloves.

For an eight-year-old and nine-year-old, getting two pairs of boxing gloves was like receiving a million dollars.

That morning, I remember going outside with Trent as each of us strapped on a pair of gloves. We were just having fun, hitting each other in the shoulder or the abdomen and trying to block one another's punches, but then Trent channeled his inner Muhammad Ali and swung at my face. He connected, too, busting my lip right open. Shocked, I wiped my lip with my arm and noticed I was bleeding substantially. In a moment of fury, not wanting to be outdone by my younger brother, I swung right back and—*boom*—punched him square in the temple. Trent immediately dropped to the ground. I didn't think I had hit him that hard, but apparently I had.

I peered over him as he lay on the ground. I could have started the ten-count.

"Trent?" I said. "Buddy, you all right?"

No response.

"Trent?" I said. "C'mon, man, wake up."

Again, no response.

He was unconscious; I had knocked him out.

So then, like any logical kid, I dragged Trent into the house, made sure my parents weren't around, and continued to drag him all the way to the bathroom. I then turned on the shower and dipped him under the ice-cold water.

Still no response.

I dipped Trent into the water again, and he finally snapped out of his unconscious state.

"Whoa, what happened?" Trent asked me, glassy eyed and confused.

"Remember our boxing gloves?" I asked.

"Yeah," he said.

"Do you want those to get taken away?"

"No," he replied.

"Okay," I said, "so you and I don't get in trouble and get our gloves taken away, we'll tell Mom and Dad that I bit my lip and you ran into a pole. Sound good?"

"Sounds good," he said.

The reason I share this is because these were the kinds of stories we were all thinking about as Christmas approached. Whether it was the routine of going to Nana's or the funny memories of Christmases past, it was painful to think about Nana buying one less pair of pajamas to give us on Christmas Eve or not being able to exchange gifts with Trent on Christmas morning.

Nana knew that none of that would feel right without Trent—it would only be painful and sobering—so she insisted on taking our family on a retreat to Wyoming for nine or ten days. Needless to say, Nana is the most loving, supportive, and generous person you could ever meet. I think that everyone felt that breaking the routine would be beneficial for our emotional states, so we agreed to the trip. Our family friends, the Oakleys, came with us, too.

Traveling to Wyoming was an awesome experience in itself. It was T.J.'s and my first time flying on a plane, and we were in so much awe being up there in the clouds. It was pretty surreal, as was seeing an endless supply of snow once we landed. Born and raised in Alabama, we weren't accustomed to seeing so much "white stuff."

When we arrived in Wyoming, we rented a cabin on a ski resort and went to the slopes just about every day. My hand was broken (again), so I snowboarded while everyone else skied. The trip was a lot of fun, and it was a much healthier way to celebrate Christmas considering our vulnerable emotional state. Though it was still hard—Christmas Day, in particular—all the fun we were having in Wyoming helped take our minds off things.

And, whereas we broke our Christmas tradition in Alabama, my parents started another one. They started taking the money that they would have spent on gifts for Trent and instead spent it on Christmas gifts for a kid who was less fortunate. On teachers' salaries, my family was never rich by any means, but they seemed to go all-out for Christmas gifts. They got the child nice clothes or something worthwhile—you know, something that they would enjoy.

Their generosity deeply impacted me. It didn't change the reality that they were hurting—it was easy to see they were wrestling with unbearable pain—but their sufferings didn't stop them from impacting someone else. Their pain didn't make them inward-focused, as it often does for people; if anything, it made them more outward-focused. The temptation, it seems, is for hardship or pain to make us immobile—incapable of moving on or focusing on anything other than our shattered lives. As Paul Young writes in his book *The Shack*, "Pain has a way of clipping our wings and keeping us from being able to fly. And if it's left unresolved for very long, you can almost forget that you were ever created to fly in the first place."

When we take tiny steps, however, and think about serving others—even in the pits of our pain—the glory of God's grace is revealed in profound ways. It is in this process of resolving our pain, while trusting and resting in God's love, that we learn to fly once more.

The evil one hoped that my family's pain would destroy my parents, but because of their willingness to obediently say yes to God amidst their pain, God used and is still using their sufferings and Trent's legacy for good.

8
Home Runs and Angels

"All is grace."
~Brennan Manning, author of *The Ragamuffin Gospel*

Winter passed, and before we knew it, the anniversary of Trent's death was upon us. I had enjoyed playing basketball with Dad coaching in the winter, and I was enjoying playing baseball with my Uncle Darryl coaching in the spring. None of it was as fun as football, but they were still sports to play—healthy distractions.

As April 1 approached, Mom wrote something pretty profound in her journal, something I would like to share.

She had been writing in her pink plastic journal over the course of the year, and I think that writing helped her sift through some of her thoughts and feelings. Experiencing such loss was something none of us had dealt with before, so it required healthy forms of expression for each of us. Without a positive form of expression in the thick of pain, those who are hurting will inevitably feel stagnant, unable to heal.

Starting at the front of the journal, Mom wrote about the things she was thinking and feeling; starting in the back of the journal, she wrote down memories of Trent that she didn't want to forget—like the last time they went to the grocery store together, for example.

Around the one-year anniversary, Mom wrote an entry about Paul Young's novel *The Shack*, a book she was reading at the time. The work of fiction is about one man's encounter with the Trinity—the Father, Son, and Holy Spirit—as he copes with the abduction and death of his daughter. It's easy to see why the plot of this book resonated with Mom. *The Shack* isn't a true story, but Mom identified with the main character because he too had lost a child. And, like herself, he too was trying to find God in the valley of the shadow of death.

Mom was especially moved by the part in the book when God introduces the main character (Mack) to Jesus and describes Jesus as the one who was counting Mack's tears. This scene reminded Mom of Psalm 56:8, which she wrote in her journal: "You have kept count of my tossings; put my tears in your bottle. Are they not in your book?"

All this might not explain why we suffer, but it does reveal how important our suffering is to Him. His love for us, all of us, is such an intimate love that He counts each and every falling tear. He records them on a scroll and meets us in our despair. This compassion and grace is a beautiful mystery that can help sustain us in our pain.

The week of Trent's anniversary (Tuesday, April 1, 2008) was a busy one. The day before Trent's anniversary, Mom, Dad, T.J., and I hopped in the car and drove to Trent's gravesite. We laid flowers on his headstone and each took a moment to pray and reflect.

His memorial looked a lot different than it had a year before. First, months before the anniversary, Nana had a wooden bench placed next to his headstone. It wasn't uncommon for her or my parents to visit the cemetery and sit on that bench for hours at a time. I didn't do this very much, but they said it was peaceful. Second, whereas Trent had a flat headstone the day he was buried, my family had commissioned a nice granite, vertical headstone six months after his death. Mom wanted his memorial to be vibrant, just like he was—not dark and gloomy like other parts of the cemetery.

On one side of the headstone, carved in bold, golden lettering, one word per line, were these words:

NEVER,
NEVER
QUIT

Below that—in smaller, gold lettering—was the verse that was on Trent's card in his pocket:

FORGETTING WHAT IS BEHIND AND STRAINING TOWARD WHAT IS AHEAD, I PRESS ON TOWARD THE GOAL TO WIN THE PRIZE FOR WHICH GOD HAS CALLED

ME HEAVENWARD IN CHRIST JESUS.

PHILIPPIANS 3:13–14

My family wanted one side of the headstone to textually resemble the card that was found in his pocket whenever he died. It reminded us of where we had been in the depths of our journey (when we found the card) but also where we were going (pressing on toward the goal) and where Trent already was (heaven).

On the other side of the three-inch-thick headstone was a centered oval-shaped picture of Trent in a turquoise polo and a light-blue under-shirt—his seventh grade school photo. Below his photograph, in the same golden lettering, were the words:

TRENT McDANIEL
MORTON
MAY 4, 1994
APRIL 1, 2007
WAITING ON MY FAMILY
AND FRIENDS IN HEAVEN

I honestly don't remember much about visiting his grave that day. As I've mentioned, I think my darkest memories were naturally sup-pressed in order to cope and keep my head on straight. I do remember my dad mentioning that we would all be buried beside Trent. If you visited Trent's grave today, you would notice a large area blocked off to the right of his grave—for Mom, Dad, T.J., and me. It's weird to stand over Trent's grave and know that we are all going to be buried there one day, but at the same time, it's a reminder to live as meaningful a life as I possibly can with the time I have been given.

As I stood at his grave around the anniversary of his death, I had a hard time believing it had already been a year—the slowest year of my life and the fastest year of my life. I don't expect that to make sense, but that's how it felt. I'd trade anything just to have one more day with him. I couldn't help but think about how, if Trent were still alive, he'd be finishing his eighth grade year and joining me for spring training on the football field in a few weeks. Our time had finally come to be reunited on the field.

Visiting Trent's grave was something that I normally tried to do alone. I'm kind of weird like that. On any anniversary or holiday, I would go there with my family, but any other time, I'd go on my own. I just didn't like to be upset around other people.

The next day, Trent's anniversary, T.J. and I both had baseball games that evening after school.

Before my game, I went to the Little League fields for T.J.'s game. The community had organized a beautiful memorial, and they revealed a plaque featuring a picture of Trent to be on display at the diamonds. It is still hanging there today. They also had T.J. throw the first pitch—him on the mound, me squatting behind the plate, just as Trent and I used to do.

I then went to the high school field for our varsity game against Jemison High School. Now, I was never a great baseball player, especially when it came to hitting. My teammates would sometimes make fun of me because it seemed like I always did one of two things: strike out or hit a home run. I might strike out 80 percent of the time, but whenever I made contact, it was usually a good result.

What had already been an emotional day became a more emotional day. In the third inning, Jeremy took a pitch and knocked it over the outfield wall. Then in the fourth, I took the first pitch of the inning, a heater, and blasted it over the left-field wall.

Two home runs.

By two of Trent's family members.

On the anniversary of his death.

As I rounded the bases, it felt like the moment was unfolding in slow motion. I didn't want it to end. The people in the stands, understanding the significance of our home runs on that particular day, were all standing up and cheering—not for me, but for Trent. Baseball was not even my favorite sport, but baseball was *Trent's* favorite sport. That's what made it so special. For some people in the community, the last memory they had of Trent was his no-hitter and 4-for-4 hitting performance on the opening day of Little League, one year before. His assistant coach, Heath Luvert, had told him to play that game like it was his last; Trent did, and it was. And for most, the last time they ever saw

Trent was at his visitation or funeral, as he lay there, eternally at rest, forever at peace, wearing his middle school Choctaw baseball uniform.

Hitting the home run felt similar to my first high school touchdown earlier that spring. I saw people standing and cheering and taking pictures with their cameras as I rounded the bases—but I couldn't hear anything. It had all gone silent.

I tagged home plate and pointed to the sky, and my teammates surrounded me, jumping up and down. The first person to embrace me was Jeremy. We both had tears in our eyes. It is difficult to explain, but it was almost as if Trent—his cousin, my brother—was in our midst. His spirit was very much alive.

As we all walked back to the dugout, Coach Hobson put his arm around me and said, "That one was for Trent."

9
Adopting the Mantra

"If you believe in yourself and have dedication and pride—
and never quit—you'll be a winner. The price of victory is
high but so are the rewards."

~Bear Bryant, Alabama head football coach (1957–1983)

This is where things speed up.

I'm not going to go into the details of each football game or individual Choctaw football memory because I don't want this to sound like a highlight reel or a sports story. My goal today is the same as it's always been—to inspire people through my brother's legacy and to encourage people through the things I've experienced. Football just happens to be in the middle of it.

Spring training for football brought with it a strange, paradoxical feeling.

On one hand, it felt good to be back playing a sport in which I thought I might have a future. Out of football, basketball, and baseball, it was football that showed the most promise for me during my freshman year, and it was the sport I enjoyed the most. Football lit a fire within me, and it was a great way to focus my attention and energy.

At the same time, I also knew I was in the spring when Trent and I were supposed to be athletically reunited. What helped fill the void was that I felt that football had the potential to become my platform. Trent's legacy could shine through me. He might not have been next to me physically on the field, but I had an opportunity to encourage people from a spiritual standpoint through the legacy Trent had left.

Heading into spring training before our 2008 campaign, out team knew that expectations were going to be high. We hadn't lost much talent. We had even more talent coming up. And we wanted to make a statement not just to our community but to the entire state of Alabama. Our goals were high. Having made it to the first round of the playoffs the year before, we wanted to make it further my sophomore year and make a splash on the statewide scene.

We also had a new coach, Mike Battles. Coach Battles had blondish, gray hair, and talked with a deep Southern accent and a raspy voice. Whereas Coach Burns was a little more laid back and soft-spoken in his approach to the game, it was easy to see early on that Coach Battles was going to be a tough coach. Whatever it took. Whatever it took to win.

I met Coach Battles for the first time earlier that spring when he called for an after-school team meeting in Bibb County's lunchroom. Getting a new coach is always kind of nerve-racking because you never know if he is going to utilize you the same way as the previous coach. Different systems and styles require different personnel and skill sets.

Upon arriving at the meeting, I noticed that Coach Battles was all business. He was dressed in a suit and tie, and it was obvious by his demeanor that he was a man who was confident, who was serious about winning, and who demanded respect.

Before the meeting started, he stopped me and said, "Are you Taylor Morton?"

"Yes, sir. I am," I said.

"We've got big plans and opportunities for you," he replied.

What he said made me feel good because it gave me confidence that my role on the team wasn't going to change much.

In fact, it was only going to get better.

Upon entering spring training, the opportunity arose for me to switch my #22 jersey that I wore throughout my freshman season with a #45 jersey in memory of Trent.

Each time I slipped on my #45 purple Bibb County Choctaws practice jersey that offseason, I was reminded of Trent's last baseball game and how he had played it like it was his last. I was challenged to do the same every day.

I felt like I was wearing his legacy on my back.

Coach Battles certainly made a statement once practice began. If you wanted to be on the team, you had to be willing to work hard. He was all business. Football was fun, but it was also a job. He was the boss, and he had high expectations for all his employees. I believe he had us working harder than any other team in the state.

One of the primary men behind our conditioning was the strength and conditioning coach, Jerome Mitchell. Coach Mitchell was a young guy with long, trendy dreadlocks. He told us that if we won State, he would let us shave them—quite the motivation because those things were really cool-looking. He was more mellow and laid back than Coach Battles, but he really knew his stuff when it came to weight lifting and exercise. Coach Battles's approach to the game, combined with Coach Mitchell's knowledge for lifting and exercise, led us to believe that we were the strongest, fastest, best-conditioned team in the state of Alabama. Though we might not have been the most talented team in the state, we believed we could outwork anyone. Coach always told us, "Talent is great, but when talent decides not to work, hard work beats talent."

As businesslike as things might have been on the field, Coach was also a genius at helping us grow closer as a team off the field. This is difficult to do when there are fifty-plus football players on the team, but by the time we made it through spring and summer conditioning, we all felt like brothers.

During the summer, Coach would often have us over to his house for cookouts and pool parties, and it was easy to tell that, as much as he cared about winning and becoming a better football team, he cared about us as young men more than anything. He was intimidating on the field but extremely personable off the field.

Everything about Coach's program bred selflessness, whether that was putting your teammate before yourself on the field or volunteering in the community. It wasn't uncommon for Coach to plan a weekend activity for us as a team that involved volunteering in Centreville. He wanted us to be in touch with the real struggles of people in the community and do whatever we could to help them.

My sophomore season was a step in the right direction both for myself and for our team. Zac Stacy, in his senior season, was the linchpin in our fluid, high-octane offense that Coach Battles had established in his first season as head coach. Overall, we averaged 39 points per game that year and showcased an offense that had to have been fun for our fans to watch. I think that being bumped down from 5A to 4A helped us, too. This was a good, fair move for us because the schools in 5A had grown to become significantly larger than us in recent years.

Overall, we finished the year with a 10-1 regular season record and an undefeated 6-0 record at home. After making it to the first round of the playoffs the year before, we advanced to the second round of playoffs in 2008, falling to Lincoln High, who went on to win the state championship.

What was neat for me on a personal level was that my teammates began adopting "Never, Never Quit" as their slogan throughout the season. Whether it was an excruciating practice in the summer heat, making a mistake in a game, or trying to mount a comeback, we often uttered those three words in order to push, challenge, and encourage one another as teammates.

I wasn't the first one who started saying it, either—someone else did. The first time I heard the phrase uttered in practice, I couldn't help but think to myself, "Whoa, did I just hear what I think I heard?" And, whereas we might have said it to inspire one another on the football field, everyone also knew the story behind those three words. It was humbling for me to realize that it wasn't just me playing for Trent—it was the entire team. Though I lost my biological brother, I felt like I had gained fifty more.

The remainder of my sophomore year, every other aspect of my life seemed to reflect the football season, meaning that everything was generally moving in the right direction. Emotionally. Spiritually. Myself.

My family. Everything. The holidays and anniversaries were still hard, but they were becoming progressively easier to handle.

That first year, nothing felt right without Trent, but, as much as it hurts to say, life without him eventually began to feel normal for me. I settled into my new reality and accepted what that new reality was. There will always be a hole that can't be filled, but when you wake up every day to the same void in your heart, time forces you to accept that it's there, and you begin to construct your life around it. Living with a void became my new normal.

As things became more normal, I also found myself talking a bit more about Trent and my own personal journey in the wake of his passing. As nervous as I might have been when I spoke at Trent's funeral, I began to discover that I actually enjoyed sharing my story because of its ability to bring people hope. I was even asked to speak a couple times at school and church. It was shocking to me that I was asked to stand in front of people and share my story, but I took it as a sign that maybe this was one of the ways I'd be able to inspire others through Trent's legacy. Most importantly, it was an opportunity to share my faith and impact people through my family's sufferings, just as my parents had done with the scholarship fund after Trent passed or what they had done with the money for Trent's Christmas gifts. I wanted to meet people where they were because that's what God had done for me. I wanted to bring a message of hope because that's what God had brought me. And I wanted to help people start a new day because that's what God had done in my life and was continuing to do in my life.

Maybe God was using me, just as I had prayed that day on my bedroom floor.

As for my family, I felt like God continued to strengthen them throughout the year as well. Don't get me wrong; Trent's passing definitely had some long-term effects on how my parents raised T.J. and me. My social life, for example, was much more controlled than it once was, despite the fact I was in high school and was about to get my driver's license. The leash, if you will, was definitely tighter. Suddenly, I had a strict curfew, and I was expected to let my parents know where I was at all times, especially on the weekends.

These newly implemented rules never bugged me, honestly. I understood why my parents were doing what they were doing. Having been so blindsided by Trent's tragedy, it was completely natural for them to be more concerned about our whereabouts and what we might be doing with our friends. Before losing Trent, death felt like a farfetched idea; however, once he died so unexpectedly, death became tangible, and it seemed like it could happen to anyone at any moment in any day. Whereas a lot of people venture through life feeling invincible, we felt that life was fragile.

One reason why I didn't mind the social boundaries and tighter leash was that I wasn't all that social. It's not like I was a hermit or anything like that—I enjoyed spending time with my friends at school or with my teammates after school—but I didn't have a ton of deep relationships with people. I might not have realized it at the time, but looking back, one change I noticed about myself during my freshman year was the group of people I let into my life. In middle school I mostly hung out with guys in my own grade, but once I got to high school, I was more drawn to an older crowd—upperclassmen, coaches, and even teachers. I wanted to be surrounded by people who had vision and goals.

For example, I had a number of mentor figures that I confided in on a daily or weekly basis: Coach Battles, David Steele (my neighbor and Sunday school teacher), Wes Cash (another Sunday school teacher), and Drew Downs (a man in his thirties who reached out to me after Trent's accident). After the accident, Drew had given me a piece of paper on which he had written his cell phone number and a quote that read, "Leaders are not born; they are made." Having mentor figures in my life was invaluable for me because it gave me some sense of direction. They were examples of men I wanted to be like—at a time when I was very impressionable.

Most might say that I became a lot more serious, perhaps less fun-loving, in the years that followed the tragedy. That's probably true. I used to be more of a goofball and free spirit. Now, I was so focused on the future and becoming a better athlete that maybe I wasn't able to enjoy the present like a normal high school student might.

Maybe focusing on the future was one of the only things that helped me move on from the past.

Spring came and went. And so did summer. All of a sudden, I was an upperclassman, entering one of the most pivotal years for a high school football player who wants to play collegiately. I hadn't been noticed by any colleges my freshman or sophomore year, so my junior year was a crucial one if I wanted to play college football, which I did.

We felt like we could do something special as a team in 2009. My freshman year, our team had advanced to the first round of the playoffs; and my sophomore year, we had advanced to the second round of the playoffs. Because we were expected to go even further my junior year, much was mentioned of the age-long curse that seemingly hung over Bibb County High School football: the belief that the Choctaws would always hit a wall in the second round of the playoffs. In its history, BCHS had never made it past the second round.

With such high expectations, it was impossible not to hear people talking about the curse. But Coach Battles tried to keep us levelheaded. He always told us, "If you can do the best with your abilities and trust the guy next to you, we've got a good chance to win." We couldn't worry about records and curses. If we focused on the little things, the big things would take care of themselves.

Though the expectations were high, there were also some questions revolving around our program at the start of the season. Many thought we might struggle with the absence of our star running back, Zac Stacy, who had graduated the year before and earned a football scholarship at Vanderbilt. As good as Zac was and despite our emphasis on the rushing game during Zac's years at Bibb, Coach Battles never seemed too concerned about our offense. After three years of playing in Zac's shadow, senior Quail Rutledge seemed to be locked, loaded, and ready.

As for me, Coach Battles still had me playing on both sides of the ball—linebacker on defense and fullback on offense. Heading into the season, I was the only player on the team who Coach utilized in a role like this. It was as if I didn't really belong anywhere, yet my speed allowed me to play just about everywhere. I was five foot eleven and weighed about 190 pounds. I think Coach wanted to take advantage of my quickness on both sides of the ball. Games were never tiring because Coach Battles had conditioned us so well, and I liked being involved in all facets of the game.

We went right to work.

After winning every single home game the year before, we followed the same trend at the start of our 2009 campaign, which included four home games in the first five weeks of the year. We won them all.

Halfway through our season, we were 5–0, our offense was averaging around 48 points per game, our defense was holding opponents to approximately 5 points per game—in between a field goal and a touchdown—and our average margin of victory was about 42 points per game. We were rolling.

But we didn't stop there. We won the next five games, too, including a nail-biter in the final week of the regular season. Overall, we finished the year with a 10–0 record, the first time Bibb County had finished the regular season undefeated since 1985. We felt like a college team. Each time we took the field, we looked like men among boys.

All in all, we averaged over 35 points per game on offense and held our opponents to under 7 points per game on defense. Like the two years before, we were perfecting the rushing game and running over our opponents, with Quail getting most of the touches. It was as if Quail filled in perfectly for Zac. At times, it seemed like we hardly ever threw the ball. But why would we? We were rushing for 300 yards every game.

Though we had accomplished something that hadn't been done in almost a quarter of a century, carding an undefeated season, our entire team knew that we had set out to do more. Reaching a milestone that hadn't been attained since 1985 was great, but we wanted to accomplish something that hadn't been done in the history of Bibb County football. We wanted to advance past the second round of the playoffs, and then we wanted to win a state championship.

Much like the season before, the phrase "Never, Never Quit" continued to pick up steam within the football program. Those three words grew to be a fixture on the team and even became one of our season's dominant themes. We said it to one another on a daily basis. And, though a lot of repetitive, motivational sayings like this can lose their meaning over time, "Never, Never Quit" never seemed to lose its gusto. It transcended so many things because someone's life was behind it.

People outside the football program began to pick up on the phrase, too. Every once in a while, I'd hear a fan yell it from the stands or a cheerleader yell it from the sidelines. I can't tell you how life-giving it is to hear people recite the same three words Trent left with us, the same three words on his headstone, the same three words that helped my family and me push through the struggle amidst the questions, doubts, and things we couldn't understand.

It wasn't just my family keeping the memory of Trent alive—everyone else was, too.

We were set to play Lincoln—the same team that had knocked us out in the second round of the playoffs the year before—in the first round of the playoffs. Honestly, I'm not sure if there was more excitement or fear from Choctaw fandom as we entered the postseason. Would we run into the same postseason troubles that Bibb County had encountered throughout its school history? Or would this year be different? Would we reverse the curse?

One good thing about the game was that we had home-field advantage. The last time we had lost a home game was November 2, 2007 of my freshman year. Coach Battles was approaching the end of his second season as head coach, and he still hadn't lost a game at home! As anxious as the postseason might have made some Choctaw fans, I think they also had a lot of confidence knowing that our successful regular season would result in hosting one, or maybe two, playoff games.

Lincoln's effort against us was noble, but it wasn't enough, and we continued the trend from the regular season, winning 36–0 and advancing to the second round of the playoffs.

We ended up hosting the second-round playoff game, too—this game against Anniston High School. Though we were coming face-to-face with our dreaded history of hitting a postseason wall in the second round, I think the fact that we were once again playing at home gave us a lot of confidence.

We breezed through that game, too, defeating Anniston 22–6 and becoming the most accomplished football team in Bibb County history. Although it felt great to make history, Coach Battles had ingrained in our minds that the goal was to do more. Unfortunately, we'd have to do it on the road, starting with Jackson High School in the third round of the playoffs.

The day we left for Jackson, it felt like a college football atmosphere at Bibb County High School. Following our pregame lunch at the school, fans lined up for half a mile to show their support. Thousands attended the pep rally held at the football field, and the cheerleaders danced to "Going to Jackson" by Johnny Cash.

Following the pep rally, we boarded nice charter buses to make the two-hour trip to Jackson. We usually traveled to games on typical yellow school buses, so riding on charter buses to the game was a neat experience, especially for a bunch of small-town country boys. As our buses pulled out of the parking lot, many of our fans followed in their own vehicles, forming a mile-long, single-file line of cars journeying together to Jackson, Alabama, all with the same goal in mind. I couldn't help but be reminded of the day of Trent's funeral when a similar line of cars followed us to Trent's gravesite. In either case, we were one community, one family.

We were trailing Jackson 25–22 with three minutes left in the game.

It had been a back-and-forth game, and we needed a defensive stop in order to get the ball back to have a chance to score to continue our historical season.

I was on the field playing outside linebacker, and I remember hearing something steadily rise in volume from the visiting bleachers, where our fans were sitting. It started soft, and then, like an approaching plane, it grew to the point that it was the only thing you could hear. In unison, one town, one family, was chanting the three words we had been saying to one another all season long, the three words that had been tattooed on my heart since Trent's passing two and a half years before:

"Never, never quit! Never, never quit! Never, never quit!"

10
Royalty

"My home is in Heaven. I'm just traveling through this world."
~Billy Graham, 20th century evangelist

"There is an endless kingdom to be enjoyed, and everlasting life to be given us, that we may live in that kingdom forever."
~John Bunyan, 17th century English writer

"You're born. You suffer. You die. Fortunately, there's a loop-hole."
~Billy Graham

Imagine taking the rush that you might get from parachuting out of a plane and combining that with the emotion you might experience on your wedding day and then combining that with the feeling you might experience when you achieve a lifelong dream—then crumble all that into one ball of emotion and put it inside you. How would that feel? I don't know what any of those things feel like—all I know is that I felt something I had never felt before when I heard the Choctaw crowd chanting, "Never, never quit!" in unison. If I could replicate that feeling, bottle it up, and sell it, I'd be a millionaire.

Despite all the things our team accomplished in 2009—the first undefeated season in twenty-five years, the first time in our history to ever make it past the second round of the playoffs—it was that moment, my brother's memory living on through the roar of the crowd in our third-round playoff game against Jackson, that was the highlight of the year for me. It still gives me chills just thinking about it.

Unfortunately, we couldn't squeeze out the victory, and Jackson defeated us 25–22. Jackson also went on to win the state championship;

it was the second year in a row that we were eliminated by a team that eventually won it all. As disappointing as losing to Jackson might have been in the moment, it was incredible to reflect on the season and think about the ways God was using Trent's legacy—and our pain—for the greater good.

Thing was, God was just getting started.

+++

Later that spring, I decided to make a decision that would stick with me for the rest of my life. I decided to get a tattoo.

I had been thinking about getting one for a while and had been fiddling with a number of designs. Though I had never really seen myself as a "tattoo guy," losing my brother and best friend led me to reconsider the idea. I wanted to do something in remembrance of Trent—something that was permanent and symbolic. One of the things I liked most about the thought of getting a tattoo was that it would forever be marked on my body, a small way to demonstrate that Trent would always be a part of me.

So on April 1, 2010, the three-year anniversary of Trent's death, I went with Mom, Dad, T.J., and my cousin Jeremy to a tattoo parlor in Alabaster, Alabama. Coming from a conservative, Baptist family, I'm sure my parents never in their wildest dreams thought they'd go *with* their son to a tattoo parlor in support of the tattoo he was about to get. (I have actually faced some judgment, particularly from people in religious circles, for having a tattoo; but perhaps we wouldn't judge one another at all if only we took the time to know one another's stories.) Not only did my parents go; they also paid for half of it.

The design I decided to go with is relatively big—about eight inches long, stretching from the top of my shoulder down my biceps and hitting about three inches shy of my elbow. Taking up the most space is a gigantic, diamond cross with a purple banner reading "Trent 45" draped over its center. Above the cross are the words "Never, Never Quit", and below the cross are the words "Phil. 3:13–14".

Most of the symbolism is fairly obvious. Trent's favorite number was 45, and it's the number I was wearing in football in remembrance of him. "Never, Never Quit" were the last three words he left for us, and it was a phrase that not only the football program had adopted but that also was gaining traction in the community. And "Phil. 3:13–14" were the verses referenced on the "Never, Never Quit" card that was found in Trent's pocket.

I know I have mentioned those verses in Philippians before; however, one of the beautiful things about Scripture is that it affects you more and more profoundly as it resonates in your heart. In each phase of my life, it seems that Philippians 3:13–14 manifests itself in different ways.

Perhaps most fundamentally, the verses have reminded me time and time again that this world is not my home. It was comforting to think about this verse in the context of Trent: God had already called him home. My mom says that we are "spiritual beings passing through a human experience"—pilgrims passing through. And because Trent had already arrived at his destination, he had gained the most important thing he could ever attain—he is with his Creator in heaven.

That's one of the reasons why I wanted the banner on my tattoo to have shades of purple. Yes, those are the school colors of Bibb County High School, where Trent and I were supposed to have some of the best years of our life together, and ironically where I felt his presence the most, there on Friday nights in my #45 uniform. But more importantly, purple is the color of royalty. Trent is in heaven with his King, Jesus. Of course, my family and I missed having Trent in our Centreville home, but Trent had already found his truest home. And why would I want to take him from that?

Around this time, Dad had a dream about Trent. He had dreamt about Trent before, but he told me this particular dream felt strangely real.

In his dream, Dad says Trent was in a place that was similar to this world but wasn't this world. This place, rather, was perfect. Dad says that he understood the place to be heaven, yet it was still a place. This would make sense since Jesus says to His disciples in John 14: "My Father's house has many rooms; if that were not so, would I have told you that I am going there to prepare a *place* (emphasis added) for you?" The setting of Dad's dream wasn't up in the clouds or anything like that; rather, it was a mysterious, tangible place. Dad cannot remember what the place looked like, but he remembers the feelings of perfection and contentment associated with it as he was dreaming.

The only other thing Dad remembers from his dream is Trent looking at him with his big, blue eyes and saying, "Dad, I'm okay."

When Dad awoke, he immediately wanted to go back to being with his son, back to where Trent was alive and well. In this place, everything was perfect. No more sin. No more sorrow. No more death.

This place, this eternal home where Trent was fully in the presence of Christ, has become one of our deepest longings as a family.

One of these days, I know I'll be with Trent in heaven. One of these days, I'll be home. But until that time comes, I'm called to take the story that God has not only given me but *blessed* me with and use it to direct people toward their truest home, which is into the loving arms of God the Father. I thank God for my story, even though it hasn't unfolded in the way I expected.

My hope and prayer is that both of the stories tattooed on my arm—Trent's legacy on earth and the fulfillment of Christ in heaven—will not only be captured on my arm through my tattoo but will also encapsulate my life and purpose here on earth.

11

A Vital Summer

"Regardless of what you want to do or who you are, fear will always see you as wholly unqualified for anything you ever dream or attempt."
~Jon Acuff, author and speaker

Ever since I was five years old and my dad took me to my first University of Alabama game, I dreamt of playing football on that field. Then again, what kid in central Alabama *doesn't* dream of one day wearing a Crimson Tide uniform? (Okay, I will concede that there are Auburn Tiger fans in central Alabama, too.)

The first college letter I received was from the University of Alabama. I got it during my junior year, and Coach Battles put it inside my locker. Seeing that envelope in my locker was a pleasant surprise— the last thing I was expecting. Inside the envelope was a flyer informing me that I was on Alabama's radar—the Crimson Tide's shoreline. It wasn't a scholarship offer or an invitation for an official visit or anything like that, but it made me aware that they had their eyes on me. I was ecstatic. I immediately took the letter and showed it to Dad. He's not one to show a whole lot of emotion, but even he said, "Whoa, that's really cool, Taylor." Having attended so many Alabama tailgates and games over the years, I think it was surreal for him to imagine one of his sons actually playing there.

I received a number of other letters throughout my junior year, too, but the only one that stuck with me came from Tuscaloosa. I was especially shocked to find out that I was the only player on the team to receive a letter from the Crimson Tide my junior season. I guess you could say this gave me some confidence that I might be able to play in a major Division I program since they had singled me out from a squad of incredible players.

Unfortunately, by the summer heading into my senior year, I was beginning to realize how difficult (and unrealistic, perhaps) it would be to attain my childhood dream of playing for the University of Alabama. Since receiving that initial letter, there had been little communication, and the school certainly wasn't pursuing me. I might have been on their radar, but they hadn't taken the next step to *really* recruit me like several smaller schools were doing. Sure, it was exciting to see that letter in my locker, but it was also kind of disappointing that my junior season performance—my best yet—might not be enough to play for UA on Saturday afternoons at Bryant-Denny Stadium.

It's not like I wasn't working hard or anything like that—it's just that Alabama is, well, Alabama. It is one of the top football programs in the country. And just because I was trying to become the best player I could possibly be didn't mean I'd get to play for whatever team I wanted. Still, I could dream.

I was invited to football camps at a number of Division I programs. Not Alabama, which was a bummer, but Division I schools nonetheless. It was weird to be already thinking about my future. It seemed to sneak up on me so quickly. In the blink of an eye, I was entering the summer before my senior year. I knew we had lots of work to do as a team on the football field that fall, but on a personal level, it was also neat to think about where I might end up after high school.

Attending those camps would turn out to be the highlight of the recruiting process for me. It was especially fun because it gave Dad and me an opportunity to spend a lot of time together, as we would drive to each school and then stay in a hotel nearby. Only God knows how many miles Dad put on my parents' car that summer. We went all around the Southeast. They knew I was following my dream and wanted to support me any way that they could.

You'd think that Dad and I might have had some really deep conversations on those drives, as much time as we were spending together, but I think we saw those trips more as an opportunity to have fun together. When you experience the trauma and loss we experienced as a family, sometimes you look for ways to escape it all, laugh a little, smile a little, and make some new memories while seeing some new places.

Sometimes Dad would say something like, "Trent would have loved this" or, "If Trent were alive, he'd be here with us," but that was honestly about as deep as things ever went. I think Dad really enjoyed going to all those schools with me, though, and it seemed to be a healthy distraction because summers were always hard. It really did feel like we were pursuing a dream together. I had a goal, and he was helping me and supporting me.

I eventually concluded that I might be crazy for wanting to play so badly at the University of Alabama. I didn't even know if I was talented enough. Plus, there were many other factors that had to line up, too. Timing. Roster spots. Position slots. Since it was looking like Alabama probably wouldn't work out, I decided to form a new goal: play football at a big, Division I school.

To be honest, I sometimes wondered if I was crazy for even thinking I could play at a Division I school. For example, when I visited a small Division I AA school in May, one of their defensive coaches bluntly approached me after my camp performance and said to me, "We don't offer scholarships to players like you," implying that I wasn't good enough to play at that level.

The coach's comment motivated me even more, but at the same time, it was kind of discouraging. Even though I was getting invited to a lot of camps and receiving letters, and although some smaller schools had offered me scholarships, I wondered if I was being unrealistic thinking that I could play at a Division I school, especially when I got such a negative reaction from a small, Division I AA school. Was I fooling myself?

Some of my doubts dissipated after I had a solid performance at the Nike Football SPARQ Combine in Mobile, Alabama, in June—a free mini-camp for high school football players who are interested in playing college football. This resulted in a respectable SPARQ rating, which is basically a score based on a player's athleticism in the following areas: speed, power, agility, reaction, and quickness (hence its name,

"SPARQ").

I felt like my individual performances from my junior season, along with our team's success, helped in getting my name out there, but my SPARQ rating seemed to solidify my legitimacy in some coaches' minds. Whereas most Division I-caliber running backs averaged a 40-yard sprint time that was around 4.8 seconds and most linebackers averaged a time that was around 5.2 seconds, I ran around a 4.6, exceeding both those marks. Following the Nike Combine, more and more letters began showing up at the football field house at Bibb County, and Coach Battles put all of them in my locker.

My favorite camp that summer was at a Division I school in Mississippi. It was there that I ran my fastest time in the 40-yard dash: 4.46 seconds. As fast as I might have felt during my freshman, sophomore, and junior seasons at Centreville, I felt like I was getting even faster. I was yet to peak, which I took as an encouraging sign.

Following the conclusion of the camp, a coach approached me, picking me out of a crowd of invitees, and started asking me questions about my future. It was obvious that he was extremely interested in me joining the program. It was exciting to feel wanted by a big school.

It was probably then that I realized I could *maybe* play college football at a Division I school. Before then, it felt like more of a far-off fantasy. It was a goal, yes, but it was difficult to comprehend. Driving back to Centreville, I had the confidence that my football career could continue at the highest college level. Maybe not at Alabama. But I felt like I could play somewhere.

It might not have been what I originally wanted, but it's all I needed.

12
History in the Making

*"The death of the Beloved bears fruit in many lives. You and
I have to trust that our short little lives can bear fruit far
beyond the boundaries of our chronologies."*
~Henri Nouwen, Dutch theologian, author, and priest

Entering the 2010 football season, there were once again some questions and uncertainties around the running back position. The previous two seasons, an argument could have been made that we had the best running backs in the state—Zac Stacy in his senior season (2008) and Quail Rutledge in his senior season (2009). Needless to say, losing players of their caliber—in a rushing offense, no less—meant there were some holes that needed to be filled.

This left the job in the backfield up to two people: my teammate C.J. Cutts and me. I would still maintain my linebacker duties on defense, but my reps would increase significantly on offense.

I didn't know it at the time, but having this opportunity to be a running back would change the direction of my future in a big, big way.

I scored the first touchdown of the season in our opener, and, just like that, we were off and running.

Just like the year before, the 2010 regular season was marked by offensive dominance and an overwhelming, suffocating defense. We won the first nine games of the regular season, averaging approximately 52 points per game under the direction of junior quarterback Jalen Goree (a great baseball player who would later be drafted by the San Diego Padres) and with a rushing offense that mirrored the previous three seasons. As for our defense, we recorded six shutouts and allowed no more than 12 points in a single game. Not bad, huh?

We lost the final game of the regular season on the road against Class 5A Pleasant Grove—our first regular season loss since my sophomore year. We entered the playoffs with a 9–1 record and would likely have home-field advantage for the first two rounds. This was encouraging because we hadn't lost a home game since my freshman season.

On a personal level, my senior season looked a lot different than my previous three seasons simply because of all the repetitions I got as a running back. My role on the team was much flashier than it had been in the past, simply because I was scoring touchdowns—the highlight of any given football game. By the end of the regular season, I probably had fifteen touchdowns or so. My first three years at Bibb, I doubt I had fifteen touchdowns combined.

Playing running back allowed me to showcase my speed in a different way than I could at linebacker, thus resulting in a diverse highlight reel for college coaches and scouts. For example, against one of our rivals, Jemison High School, in Week 4, I had a first-half rushing performance that could have made any scout drool. In our first two plays of the game, I broke free for back-to-back 40-yard runs to score a touchdown, and at the end of the first half, I took a pitch to the outside and once again broke free, this time for an 82-yard touchdown. Overall, I had about 175 yards on only 10 carries.

Combine those highlights with some of my defensive performances, say, against cross-town rival West Blocton in Week 9—an intra-county rivalry that had been renewed for the first time in twenty-seven years— and I had a full package of highlights to take to recruiters. Against West Blocton, I had a couple of rushing touchdowns along with a fumble recovery for a touchdown and an interception.

I hope I do not come across as arrogant as I mention some of these games and individual highlights. My intention is simply to show how all these opportunities to showcase my speed in different ways benefited me later on.

The 2010–11 regular season was at times emotional for my family and me. As my high school career came to a close, it was difficult to think about what those years could have been like for our family if it wasn't for that cruel day, April 1, 2007. The renowned success of the football program at Bibb County was a great distraction for all of us, but it also had touches of bitterness because we couldn't experience it with Trent. He should've been out there on the field with me for three of the most exciting years in Bibb County football history. As competitive as Trent was, he would have loved it.

The game against West Blocton in Week 9 was especially emotional because it was Senior Night. That's probably why I had one of the best performances of my high school career—because I was escaping through football like I had always done, funneling all my emotion into a game.

I talked earlier about the empty chair at our kitchen table every night—well, Senior Night brought back some of those same feelings. A number of seniors and their families were honored before the game, and Mom, Dad, and T.J. stood next to me on the field. Even three and a half years after the tragedy, it still didn't feel right being down there with just those three. Someone was missing. You could see the hole in our lives.

Over the years, it was tough to look around and see everyone else's siblings, and it was especially difficult in moments like these when it was another poignant reminder of all we had lost. Again, my point in bringing all this up isn't for the reader to feel sorry for my family or me. I am simply mentioning how it felt to stand on the field at the time. It was weird how a sense of togetherness, something so good—your whole family being at the game in support of you—can dredge up so much hurt and pain.

Though Trent could not physically be there, I was reminded soon after that his spirit was very much alive in the community. When we ran out of the tunnel that night as a team, we burst through a huge paper banner that read: "NEVER, NEVER QUIT". The crowd went wild.

It might have been a night about the seniors, but it was also a night about Trent. His memory lived on, and his legacy continued to impact people in ways that I could have never imagined.

The most memorable thing about the 2010 regular season, like the year before, was the fact that "Never, Never Quit" continued to take on a life of its own. Ever since it was chanted in the fourth quarter of our third-round playoff game the year before, it seemed like the Choctaw fan base and Centreville community had latched onto the phrase. At the beginning of the season, the booster club made shirts on which the phrase was written in big, bold letters. And at every game, home or away, it wasn't uncommon to hear the chant multiple times.

It was as if the phrase became Choctaw football's unofficial mission statement or motto. It was our rallying cry, not only because of the power of the words but most importantly because of the story behind them.

We coasted through the opening rounds of the playoffs, winning our first two games and advancing to the third round—the same round where our dreams had come to an end a year before.

Two more victories and we'd be in the state championship.

That's all we needed.

And we were determined to get there.

It was easy to see how hungry we were in the third round against Escambia County—hungry to make history and advance further than the year before, hungry to win a state championship like we had set out to do at the start of the season.

We won 35–14, Escambia's only two touchdowns coming in the final quarter.

Like the year before, we had once again made history, advancing further than any Choctaw football team.

In the locker room, Coach Battles told us, "Enjoy this one, but be ready to get back to work tomorrow." He kept us focused on the task at hand.

One more victory, and we'd have the opportunity not only to make history but to be etched in it.

Unfortunately, the season ended in a bitter fashion—against a team that would end up running away with the state championship. I'm talking about Thomasville High School, the third team in three years to go on to win State after knocking us out of the playoffs. They defeated us 38–14 and went on to beat Deshler in the state championship, finishing the season with an undefeated 14–0 record. We were outmatched, as was every team that went up against them that year. I've mentioned that we had a strong and physical team, but they took that to a whole new level. They were just the better team.

Still, it had been a great year, the best in Bibb County football history. No one could take that away from us. There were a lot of despondent players in the locker room, but, as disappointing as it was, the pain I had experienced in life helped me put wins and losses in perspective. I had already flipped the page and started looking ahead to the future. Where would I play collegiate football?

13
What If?

"The decisions you regret in life are the ones you didn't make. And you will be haunted by the question, 'What if?' Some people tried the risk and failed, but they are still satisfied because they had the courage to try. They have self-respect, even though they didn't get what they expected."
~John Maxwell, motivational speaker and author

National Signing Day is usually on the first Wednesday of February, which gave me about nine weeks to make a decision.

I was pretty sure that I had my choice narrowed down to a handful of schools. A few Division I schools offered me the position of a preferred walk-on (meaning a guaranteed spot on the team but no scholarship), and a couple Division III schools offered me partial athletic scholarships.

By this point, playing at the University of Alabama was completely out of the picture. I had gone on a number of unofficial visits that fall since my family continued going to Saturday games, but the interest wasn't reciprocal. I concluded that I wasn't good enough to play there.

That being said, I was leaning toward accepting one of the preferred walk-on opportunities at a Division I school. A couple of those schools were in the South, so saying yes would allow me to play Division I football, a dream of mine, and would keep me close to home, which was important as well. Though I received hundreds of letters during my high school career, I ignored most of the ones that came from out-of-state schools. I think moving that far away would have been really tough on my parents and me.

Still, as good as some of the opportunities were, it was difficult to feel 100 percent committed to any one school. I didn't know why. Don't get me wrong; I was excited. But for some reason, I couldn't

105

shake the thought of playing at Alabama, even though communication with them was practically non-existent.

A month from National Signing Day, I was still undecided, so we made one last desperate attempt to get Alabama to take notice of me. I say "desperate" because that's exactly what it was. Throughout the recruiting process, I had tried not to come across as overeager to play there, but we were entering crunch time.

Here's what happened. One day, Jim Oakley, the Oakley children's grandfather (we call him "Daddy Jim"), took some of my senior film on DVD over to the University of Alabama and gave it to a woman in the athletic department named Ashley. Daddy Jim asked her to get it into the hands of Alabama's secondary coach at the time, Jeremy Pruitt.

When Daddy Jim returned to Centreville, he told us that it went well, but I don't think any of us, including him, expected to hear anything back from them. This was Alabama that we were talking about. Nonetheless, it was a kind gesture by Daddy Jim, and I really appreciated it. I was a little anxious about my upcoming decision, but I believed God would lead me right where He wanted me to be.

The next day at school, I received a call on my cell phone in the middle of passing period. At Bibb, our phones were taken away if any faculty saw us using them during the school day, but I recognized that the number was from the University of Alabama, so I rushed into the bathroom to answer the call.

"Hello?" I said.

"Hey, is Taylor there?" said the voice on the other end.

"This is Taylor," I said.

"Hey Taylor, this is Patrick Suddes, head of football operations at the University of Alabama."

"Hey, Coach Suddes," I replied.

"I received your film yesterday from our defensive backs coach, Jeremy Pruitt. We showed it to Coach Saban, and we were all very impressed. We've discussed it, and we'd like to bring you on as a preferred walk-on if you're interested. We want you on the team, and we've got a spot for you if you want it."

I don't even remember the rest of the conversation.

The first person I called upon hearing the news was Dad. I called him right there in the bathroom, too. Pretty sure I was late to my next class. I don't think I cared.

"Congratulations, son," Dad said once I told him. "I'm proud of you."

All the hard work, all the traveling, all the disappointments and setbacks, and all the successes—the journey of it all—seemed to reach its crescendo at that moment. That call was what we had worked so hard for.

Over the next couple of weeks, I talked to my dad a lot about Alabama, just to make sure I was doing the right thing. They weren't offering me a scholarship, and I understood that it might be more difficult to crack into the lineup, but Alabama presented me with the opportunity of a lifetime.

"You know," I remember Dad saying one day, "if you go play at a smaller school, you might get more playing time, and you might even have a successful career, but you'll always wonder, 'What if?' If you go to the University of Alabama, you'll never have to ask yourself, 'What if?' Because you're going to be playing for one of the best college football programs in the country."

I took his advice to heart. I didn't want to look back on my life and wonder what could have been.

During this time, Daddy Jim said something that has stuck with me to this day: "You'll have a larger platform for Jesus being a walk-on at Alabama than being a star player at any other school."

+++

The whole ordeal was an interesting strand of events. In hardly no time at all, I had gone from being unsure about my future to being completely certain, from thinking my dream was out of reach to seeing it happen right in front of me, from giving up on playing for Alabama to becoming a preferred walk-on for the Crimson Tide. All because Jim Oakley drove to Tuscaloosa and gave Alabama my film one month before National Signing Day.

As is usually the case with God's plan, it was humbling to think about how unlikely it was for everything to line up the way it did. Daddy Jim dropped by Alabama on just the right day at just the right time; the right people were at Alabama on the day that he dropped by; Alabama had a roster opening that meshed with my speed and skill set; and the DVD featured a diverse highlight reel regarding my in-game speed because I was given an opportunity to play as a running back my senior season. It was as if the opportunity to play at Alabama had been perfectly and uniquely handcrafted for me.

This wasn't a huge surprise, because it is in God's very nature to care about the intricate details of our lives, as the gospel itself is incomprehensibly personal and relational. I could see God's hand in it all. There wasn't a doubt in my mind that God made all this happen—not me.

A week later after I received the exciting phone call, my family and I drove to Tuscaloosa for a meeting with Coach Suddes. We met in the team lounge of the football complex, one of the most extravagant facilities I had ever seen. Visiting the Alabama football facility for the first time was unforgettable. There was a weight room, players' lounge, hydrotherapy room, hydration stations, and even a smoothie bar. I had never seen anything like it before. What's crazy is that the football complex would improve even more three years later with a significant renovation and the addition of a brand-new weight room. At the time, though, when I stepped into the facility for the first time as a senior at Bibb County, I would have never imagined that something so elaborate could be improved even in the slightest bit.

During our meeting, Coach Suddes issued an advisory: "You have a place on the team, but it will be hard to break into the lineup as a walk-on. Just work really hard and try to earn yourself a spot on special teams first. You can do it."

As excited as I was to have a spot on the Crimson Tide, I knew it was only a step. Not a destination. A step. I had an opportunity to be a part of a team I had watched my entire life, and though this was worth celebrating and enjoying, I didn't want my journey to stop there—I wanted to *play* for the Crimson Tide on Saturday and help them win.

I had not yet arrived. In fact, now there was even more work to do.

'14
Birthed from Pain

"While other worldviews lead us to sit in the midst of life's joys, foreseeing the coming sorrows, Christianity empowers its people to sit in the midst of this world's sorrows, tasting the coming joy."

~Tim Keller, founding pastor of Redeemer Presbyterian Church in New York City

"I am certain that I never did grow in grace one-half so much anywhere as I have upon the bed of pain."
~Charles Spurgeon, 19th century English theologian

I couldn't wait to play football at the University of Alabama. Thing is, I had to graduate from Bibb County High School first.

Part of the requirement for graduating from Bibb was turning in a senior project. If you didn't turn in a senior project, they wouldn't give you your diploma, even if you had a 4.0 GPA. The project had very few guidelines, but it had to be taken seriously by the students. The purpose of the project was to create something or to serve the community in some way.

One of my classmates built a walkway from the high school to the Cahaba River. Anna Michael planted flowers in front of the school. What made the project fun for me was that it was an opportunity to work on something that I was actually passionate about. The best senior projects usually entailed a lot of work, but it was different than grinding through a typical homework assignment because I actually cared about it—not to say that I didn't care about homework, but, well, I guess you could say I didn't care all that much about homework. Sorry, Mom.

For my project, I decided that I wanted to arrange a gathering that would resemble a Christian conference. There were a number of variables that led me to this idea. First, we were approaching the fourth anniversary of Trent's death, which meant that it was once again time for our family to award the annual Trent McDaniel Morton Scholarship to a high school senior. I figured arranging an event might help raise awareness for the scholarship and might even help raise more money for the scholarship fund.

Second, I loved the idea of having an opportunity to speak to a group of people. Speaking was something that I could see myself doing in my career; I enjoyed it, and for some reason I kept getting asked to do it, mostly at youth groups or other small gatherings. Through my speaking engagements, I realized that everyone seemed to be suffering or struggling with something. Not everyone in a given room had lost a sibling, but it did seem that everyone was looking for strength or hope in their struggles. I was only a kid, but I think that the uniqueness of my story and my platform as a football player in a football-crazed region helped with the reception of my message. I was learning that God could use anyone—at any age—to turn a mess into a message and a test into a testimony, as I've heard it said.

Lastly, and perhaps most importantly, Trent had been deeply impacted at a church conference a year before his death, so I think there was personal, emotional appeal for me to organize something that could have a similar impact on someone else. My family loved the idea, too, and they told me that they would help in any way they could. We went right to work.

I decided to call the gathering "Converge Bibb." I liked the word "converge" because of its simple definition: coming together. Our mission for Converge was "to break down racial, social, and denominational barriers that hinder us from coming together and worshiping the one, true, and living God." What could we all accomplish as the body of Christ if we were one unified whole?

We decided to host the event at Four Points Baptist Church because the facility was across the road from Bibb County High School. We promoted the event through Facebook, and *The Centreville Press* even ran a story about it. We also sought sponsors for the event to cover some of our overhead costs so all the money raised at the event could go directly to the scholarship fund. Turns out, I liked working on some of the behind-the-scenes, business-type things. I found it thrilling to watch something come together and enjoyed networking with others and welcoming them to our team. What was especially fun was seeing others become genuinely excited about what we were doing.

The day of the event, we were blown away by the turnout. Over five hundred people attended—students, teachers, children, parents, members of the community, and many others.

Each person who attended received a light blue T-shirt to wear. I wanted everyone to match to symbolize our unity as one body. The T-shirt said "CONVERGE BIBB" on the front and listed all the event's sponsors on the back.

Most importantly, lives were changed at the event. Over three thousand dollars were raised for the scholarship fund, and a number of people also dedicated their lives to Christ, including one girl who said she had gotten up that morning intending to commit suicide that evening. The message of the gospel gave her the hope she needed to keep living as well as the value and acceptance in Christ she had always craved.

The only bad thing about the event was that it had to end. After seeing the way God used the gathering together of His people as an impactful and encouraging time, we couldn't help but ask ourselves the question: Why don't we keep doing this?

What started out as a senior project has blossomed, over the years, into a non-profit ministry called Converge Ministries. Each year, through Converge, we host an event that calls together the people of central Alabama. We also host a golf tournament or a 5k race to raise money for the Trent McDaniel Morton Scholarship. We try to partner with causes throughout the year that hopefully meet people in their lowest places and give them hope. As of 2015, the annual event has grown from five hundred people to *four thousand* people. One year, we raised ten thousand dollars for the scholarship fund.

Just as Bibb County's adoption of the phrase "Never, never quit" was a reminder that Trent's legacy was continuing to live on, the birth of Converge was another one of those reminders. Converge presented us with an opportunity to tell Trent's story and to point people toward a greater story—whether that was through the annual event, a golf tournament, a race, a scholarship, or the other opportunities that came along the way.

Nothing will ever be able to adequately fill the hole in our lives that the death of Trent left, but when we heard about the girl who chose not to commit suicide because she had been impacted by Trent's story and most importantly by the gospel, it encouraged us to know that Trent's death might have inspired someone to choose life. Over the years, we've heard tons of stories like this, and it's interesting to reflect on all the positive things that have come from a very negative circumstance—the tragic death of my brother.

People sometimes ask my family, "How does it make you feel that all these lives have been changed?", hinting that maybe the lives wouldn't have been changed if it weren't for Trent's death and legacy. Our response is usually something along the lines of, "It's great to see what God is doing with his legacy, but if it were up to us, we'd still rather have Trent with us today."

This might not sound like a "Christian response" when factoring in all the good things that have come from April 1, 2007, but it's the truth. I think people want us to respond to the question with something like, "All the pain is worth it" or "Trent had to die so all these lives could be changed" or "We're thankful things happened the way they did," but to respond like that would be to deny the ever-existing pain within. I lost my brother, and though it brings me great joy to hear about the impact his legacy is having, he was still my brother, and he is no longer with us. No amount of good will ever fill this void.

The truth is that God didn't need Trent to pass away to change people's lives; God can change people's lives any way He wants to. And yet, just as He allowed Trent to die, He also allows us to be a part of His redeeming plan in this world. We've learned that saying yes to being part of His redeeming plan is difficult to do in suffering because it involves a lot of incomprehensible things; however, it can also lead to incredibly impactful stories, since everyone can relate to pain and weakness. Author Paul Young puts it this way: "Grace doesn't depend on suffering to exist, but where there is suffering, you will find grace in many facets and colors." This has become the great spiritual journey for my family and me: seeing the different colors of grace in our suffering and anxiously waiting to see how God takes our brokenness and uses it to encourage someone else.

The interesting thing about Converge's existence is that it was founded out of a place of suffering. Its very foundation is pain. Though there is nothing fun about suffering, what I do find encouraging is the power that suffering has. This has been true throughout all of history. The foundation of the Christian faith is a suffering Savior. The church was founded by suffering disciples, and the church expanded under intense oppression and persecution. Every great movement in our country's history has involved some sort of suffering.

Though I wish Trent were still alive today, I cannot ignore the fact that something beautiful was birthed in our pain, and for that I am very thankful.

15
T-Town

"It's okay to not be okay."
~Dominique Voillaume, French monk who served the poor

*"In Alabama, there are three classes of people: Alabama
Crimson Tide fans, Auburn Tiger fans, and atheists."*
~David Shepard, author of *Bama, Bear Bryant and the Bible*

Once the Converge Bibb conference was complete, things began to happen very quickly.

The third week of April, with a month or so left in my senior year, I attended A-Day (Alabama's annual spring football game) with my parents, T.J., and Jeremy. Though most of Alabama's big-time scholarship players made their commitments on National Signing Day in February, many of the preferred walk-ons were invited to sign their letters of intent two months later on A-Day.

The actual signing that morning was a low-key ordeal. All I did was drop by the indoor practice facility and quickly sign my letter of intent. There were a number of other housekeeping things that I needed to complete while I was on campus, and since T.J. and Jeremy were such big Alabama fans, I think they enjoyed tagging along with me throughout the day. They were like kids in a candy store getting to see some of the ins and outs of the football program.

The best part of the day, of course, was attending the game. I had attended A-Day before as a fan—my family and I usually went every year—but it was completely different attending the game and enjoying the day's festivities as a future player.

Instead of sitting in the stands at the game, I got to watch the game from the sidelines with some of the other signees and incoming freshmen. During the game, I remember scouting out the competition and trying to figure out whom I might be competing against for a position once I officially started practicing with the team. It was weird to even consider something like this, but at the same time, it felt exactly right.

A week and a half later, however, playing football at the University of Alabama became the last thing on my mind.

It was a Wednesday—April 27, 2011—and I remember attending a National Honor Society ceremony right after school. First off, going to NHS functions always felt a little ghostly because my last picture taken with Trent had been at an NHS ceremony—Trent to my left in a turquoise-colored polo, staring blankly into space; T.J. to my right wearing a baby-blue Upward basketball T-shirt and smiling (surprisingly) for the camera; and me in the middle wearing a white shirt and black tie, looking awkward as usual; the purple-and-gold-painted brick of the middle school gymnasium behind us. Today, I have the photograph framed and sitting on the desk in my room.

What made my senior-year National Honor Society ceremony especially eerie was what happened an hour away; as the ceremony came to a close, we learned that a serious EF4 tornado had touched down in Tuscaloosa. I'll always remember the teachers turning on the televisions at the high school and watching the horrific footage with my friends as it unfolded live on national television—one of the most terrifying things I've ever seen.

When I returned home, there was a report that a tornado had also touched down in Eoline, Alabama, just eight minutes away from Centreville, so my family and I went to the Kyzers' house next door, where we routinely went during bad weather, and huddled together in their basement. Nothing ever touched down in Centreville, but over the course of the next day, we heard details about the Tuscaloosa tornado: forty-plus people were killed (six of them being Alabama students), hundreds were injured, and over 10 percent of the city's structures were destroyed. It was the worst tornado the state of Alabama had ever seen.

The next week, Bibb County High School gave its students an opportunity to go to Tuscaloosa during the school day to help with the relief effort. I went with a number of my friends, including Jeremy.

Driving into Tuscaloosa felt like pulling into a war zone. It looked like a big bomb had gone off. Debris everywhere. People walking around, lost and distraught. It was far from the vibrant, happening city I was used to experiencing on Saturdays at Crimson Tide football games. Walking along those streets felt apocalyptic. Getting Tuscaloosa back to where it once was felt like a daunting, impossible task.

The end of my senior year was emotional, to say the least.

First, the tornados in Tuscaloosa happened in April. Then graduation happened in May, and it brought up some of the same feelings as Senior Night—that something was off in the absence of Trent.

To be honest, part of me felt as if I should have moved on from the pain by then. It had been four years, after all. However, one of the most encouraging things someone ever said to me was, "It's okay to never be okay about Trent. We are human beings. We're not supposed to be okay."

This was a freeing revelation because it allowed me to move forward knowing that I shouldn't feel guilty for sometimes feeling upset. I was once more reminded of my three favorite words: "Never, never quit." Never quitting did not imply that the goal was being okay; the goal was being resilient. In his book *Resilience*, Navy SEAL Eric Greitens writes: "Pain can break us or make us wiser. Suffering can destroy us or make us stronger. Fear can cripple us, or it can make us more courageous."

We cannot always control how despair might blindside us. Resilience, however, I could pursue. As the character Rocky Balboa says in *Rocky Balboa* (2006), "It ain't about how hard you hit. It's about how hard you can get hit and keep moving forward. How much you can take and keep moving forward. That's how winning is done!" My goal was to let God use me in my present form, to claim my blessessedness each day and not buy into the lie that I was a victim, and to approach each moment with hope in my soul and not bitterness in my heart.

Most of my friends in my senior class had one last summer vacation before going off to college, but my summer "vacation" only lasted three days. That's because I was expected to report to Tuscaloosa seventy-two hours after graduation to begin my freshman classes and to start conditioning with the 2011–12 Crimson Tide.

Tuscaloosa might only have been a forty-minute drive away from Centreville, but going there felt like sailing off to an island. In Centreville, I was a star football player who had a story that was known by the entire town. In Tuscaloosa, I would be starting all over; no one knew if I was a good football player or not, and no one knew or cared about my story. I had to be fine with that.

As unfamiliar a feeling as this might have been, the thought of starting over brought with it a lot of excitement. I was setting out on a new adventure—beginning a new chapter in my life. I had an opportunity to earn my stripes at a perennial football powerhouse, and I was ready to earn them, one at a time.

The only guy on the team I knew was Dustin Ellison. He was a fellow freshman preferred walk-on who had played quarterback at Monroe Academy, a couple hours south of Centreville. Nana and Dustin's father happened to work together, so when they found out that Dustin and I would both be playing for Coach Saban at Alabama, they connected us, and Dustin and I struck up a friendship in the spring of our senior years.

Dustin and I decided to room together in the summer. Since we were both in a new place on a new team—and on the bottom of the food chain—I think we knew it would help to have one another.

I arrived in Tuscaloosa on a Tuesday and had one day to get settled in before the first run as a team on Wednesday. All I could think about was football; I was anxious to begin.

Most of Tuesday was spent at the Alabama football complex. The first thing I did was drop by the front desk to get my thumb scanned so I could have access to the facility—yes, with a thumbprint—anytime that I wanted. For a small-town, country boy, I felt like I had stepped into the world of *Star Trek* or something. Whatever the case, it was cool, and it was crazy to think I could go to the football complex whenever I wanted—any day of the week at any time of the day or night.

While at the facility, freshman scholarship players and preferred walk-ons (there were about twenty of us) had to attend a couple classes on NCAA rules and regulations: don't bet on your team, don't sell sports memorabilia, don't accept money from fans or boosters, and other stuff like that. I think I signed about a thousand papers and consent forms that day.

Most of our meetings were conducted in the players' lounge, with its leather chairs, seventy-inch LCD screens, and innovative technology. Strength and conditioning coach Scott Cochran was the only coach who was around at this point in the summer because the NCAA prohibits head coaches and assistants from working with players until the start of summer training camp. Strength and conditioning coaches are exempt from that rule. This is one reason many of us formed a deep relationship with Coach Cochran: he was around us more than any other coach.

I had heard stories about Coach Cochran—stories about his intensity, his motivation tactics, and his distinct, booming, crackly voice. The day of our meetings, however, Coach Cochran was in his tamest of states. He wasn't in the weight room or on the field. He was simply overseeing boring protocol for the newcomers. That day, he didn't seem all that scary. This would change.

"Get your minds ready, and get your minds right," he calmly told us. "If you want to play for the Crimson Tide, you have to follow the procedures, rules, and regulations. By being here, you are expected to put Alabama football over everything else. This is now your job."

Later that day, we received our gray, Nike Dri-FIT workout clothes to wear the next day at practice for our first team run. The shirt had a crimson-colored image of a football on the front with "BAMA" above the image and "FOOTBALL" below the image. We also received our workouts shoes, cleats, and socks—all Nike.

As neat as it was to get my workout clothes and officially become a part of the Crimson Tide family, I was too anxious about the next day of conditioning for any of it to sink in.

Dustin and I were so nervous the night before that we hardly slept. What would the first day of practice be like? Were we prepared? What would it take? How bad was it going to be?

I can't imagine that we slept more than an hour.

Attending my Western Civilization class the next day felt even longer than the night before. The class was three hours long and seemed to drag into eternity. Football completely consumed my mind. I struggled to eat anything at all that day, so I just drank as much water and Gatorade as possible, since I knew I'd need it. It was 104 degrees outside, and the heat index was around 110 degrees. Perfect running conditions.

Finally, at around four o'clock, I drove to the facility. From there, I went to the locker room and found my locker, which had more Nike gear inside. I quickly put on my gear in an awkward locker room full of strangers. I remember Aaron Joiner, a junior offensive lineman, approaching all us nervous walk-ons and saying, "You guys ready for this?" in sort of a foreboding way.

This is going to be awful, I thought to myself.

By five o'clock, there were over 130 players on the practice field. Most were returning players who were laughing and smiling, enjoying being back on the field with their family. Looking back, it's funny to think that I was a pipsqueak freshman sharing the field with some of the best players in the country like offensive lineman Barrett Jones and running back Trent Richardson, to name a couple. At the time, however, you don't think about things like that. You're simply there in the moment.

While some of the star recruits might have felt looser or more confident, the walk-ons and those trying to make the team were definitely more quiet and awkward. There was a sense of pride in joining such an elite group, but there was also the pressure of knowing you had to prove yourself. I wanted to start proving myself. I was ready to get going.

In minutes, strength and conditioning coach Scott Cochran came out onto the field and began setting the tone for the season. His manner was much different than the day before. Immediately, everyone there understood that the burly, blond-haired man standing in front of us was going to put us through some sort of purgatory for the next several months.

Right away, it was easy to see that Coach Cochran had a distinct personality. He had the most interesting demeanor and voice—sounding completely normal one second and super intense the next second. Anytime he got excited or angry—or felt any type of emotion for that matter—he would belt something in a deep, raspy voice that seemed to come straight from the pit of his stomach. It was as if he had something intense living inside him, trying to burst out of his body.

I know I mentioned earlier that the fact that I was going to be playing for Alabama hadn't settled in at the time. Well, things settled in quickly once we started running.

Coach Cochran put us through a rigorous running workout that consisted of sprinting eighty yards as hard as we could, then jogging thirty yards into the back of the end zone, then sprinting eighty yards in the opposite direction, and then jogging thirty more yards in order to recuperate. He called them "blocks."

"Full speed every time!" Coach Cochran yelled. "If I catch you slacking, we'll start over!"

Within minutes of running, we had all removed our shirts in an attempt to cool down. Those efforts were futile. We were like eggs sizzling in a pan. It was pointless for us to even put on sunscreen before practice because we sweat it all off in no time. One thing was certain: we were going to bake until we were burnt.

While running blocks, I remember looking to my right at one point and seeing Trent Richardson sprinting next to me in the grueling heat. A guy I had watched throughout high school was now my teammate. That was pretty crazy, but I quickly got over it. There was no time for star-gazing; it was time to get to work.

Coach Cochran made us run sixteen blocks the first practice—all in the blistering heat. A lot of the newcomers puked, and some walk-ons were cut that day. It was obvious that the process of weeding out talent had already begun. Coach Cochran didn't want to hear any excuses or complaining—he wanted perfection. It was insane. Just the way he liked it. Welcome to the Crimson Tide.

I might not have puked or anything, but I walked off the practice field that day completely exhausted. I was achy and dehydrated, and I could tell that I was sunburnt.

Following practice, I went to the nutrition bar to hydrate and replenish the vitamins I had lost. I felt weak, but I also felt the accomplishment of surviving my first practice with the Crimson Tide. It wasn't easy, but I was confident that I belonged on the team.

That's when Coach Cochran approached me. He looked me square in the eyes, as seriously as you can imagine, and said, "You better pick it up or you won't last long here."

16
'It's Only Pain'

"I consider that our present sufferings are not worth comparing with the glory that will be revealed in us."
~Romans 8:18

"It's only pain."
~Scott Cochran, Alabama strength and conditioning coach

Coach Cochran's words lit a fire beneath me.

You better pick it up or you won't last long here.

I knew he'd be watching to see how I responded to his challenge.

Following our initial team run on the first day of practice on Wednesday, we entered our summer, two-a-day training plan for the rest of the week. We dove right into it.

Monday through Thursday in summer conditioning, we had the option to either run at six o'clock in the morning or at five o'clock in the evening before our team lifting session. Most of us got up early and ran at six o'clock in the morning because it was about twenty degrees cooler outside.

As hard as I worked at the first day of practice on Wednesday, I pushed myself to places I never imagined I could go on Thursday. I knew Coach Cochran had his eye on me (Coach Cochran had his eye on everyone), and I wanted to prove to him that I had what it took to play at the University of Alabama. I knew I probably wasn't the next Trent Richardson, but whatever I lacked in talent, I wanted to make up for in passion and will. I wanted Coach Cochran to see that, and I think he did.

Surviving Thursday's practice meant that I had one more day left in my first week of conditioning. It was a short week since we had started practice that Wednesday, but it definitely didn't feel like a short week.

Our sessions on Wednesday and Thursday were the most intense conditioning I had ever experienced. And we were just getting started.

On Fridays, I learned that we didn't have a choice to do a morning or an afternoon run. Everyone ran and worked out together—as a team—at six in the morning. Friday practices ended up being my favorite practice days because it was fun being together with the team. That first Friday, however, I had no idea what to expect.

We went to the practice fields, and Coach Cochran took us through some agility drills. They were pretty fun and weren't all that tiring. Of course, the morning became much more difficult after that. Following the agility drills, we all boarded buses and were dropped off at Bryant-Denny Stadium. It's a peaceful thing to be at Bryant-Denny Stadium in the early hours of the morning, with the sun rising and all the colors in the sky, but that peace quickly fades when you hear Coach Cochran's booming voice.

"We're gonna run ten stadiums!" he belted. "Up and down counts as one! If I see *one* of you slacking, if *one* of you stops running, then the whole team will have to start all over! Yea-yea-yea-yeaaaaaaaa!"

It was only my third day of practice, but I was quickly learning that "Yea-yea-yea-yeaaaaaaaa!" was one of Coach Cochran's many signature phrases. I tell you, the man has passion and enthusiasm flowing through his veins. He is never lacking for energy, nor does he need anything to give him energy—coffee, sleep, etc. He only needs football and his players.

After our stadium runs—running all the way to the top of Bryant-Denny and all the way back down as fast as we possibly could ten times in a row—we boarded the buses again and were dropped off at the weight room, where Coach Cochran led each group of players in their lifting workout for the day. I was with the safeties and defensive backs. Once we completed our lifting workout, we were done for the week. I had made it through my first week with the Crimson Tide—and had done it without passing out or puking my brains out.

When I had driven to Tuscaloosa four days before, I hadn't known what to expect. But after three grueling days of workouts, playing for the Crimson Tide was beginning to feel good and normal and right.

From there, throughout the rest of May and into June and July, practices only got crazier and harder. At Alabama, there was no such thing as "coasting." Every day of training was a grind. Coach Cochran expected you to push yourself to the limit and then past the limit and then past the limit again.

Unlike high school, in which kids would sometimes join a sports team just to have fun and maybe have a good experience along the way with friends, there wasn't a single person on the Crimson Tide team who was there just to have fun. How can I say something like that? Well, because it wasn't fun . . . at all. It was meaningful and rewarding. But it sure wasn't fun. Coach Cochran's priority wasn't for his players to have a good time. His priority was to help us become better men and to position us to win a national championship. In the messy, straining, painful process of all that, we became closer as a team, which *was* fun because we were all working hard—together.

I've heard that it's important to surround yourself with people you want to be like, and this was what happened as I ventured through my first summer of conditioning at Alabama. Those whose talent or passion or work ethic didn't align with the overall culture of the program were weeded out, allowing those of us who were left to work together toward a common goal. If you didn't go to bed every night able to admit, "I left it all out there on the field today," then there was a good chance that you were about to get cut from the team.

Coach Cochran's conditioning tested our very cores. If we allowed ourselves to quit in something like a football practice, then maybe we would quit on a marriage or a job later on in our lives when things got difficult. If we didn't go all in on something like football, then maybe we wouldn't give our all in the classroom or for a boss or even for ourselves. Our work ethic and will, under the intensity of one of the most passionate strength and conditioning coaches in the country, was a direct reflection of who we were as people.

Playing football under these conditions isn't for everyone, and there's nothing wrong with that, but if you've committed to play at a place like the University of Alabama, then it's expected that your drive will align with the prestige of the program. Continuing to sprint as hard as we could in the blistering heat—when we had nothing left to give and had sunburned skin and legs without feeling—was a reflection of who we were as men.

+++

Our growth as men was one of the cornerstones of Coach Saban's program. Football was merely the tool the coaches used to help develop us into young men who could enter the world and have a positive effect on society.

A great example of this was Alabama football's response that summer to the tornado damage.

Each weekend throughout the summer, we players were encouraged to be out in the community doing whatever we could to help Tuscaloosa—whether it was cleaning up debris or spending time with the victims of the tragedy. Though Coach Saban wasn't permitted to be with us yet, it was obvious that this intentional focus on something that went far beyond football came straight from the top. Coach was heavily involved in the community throughout the summer, and anytime he wasn't in Tuscaloosa, he was out on the road raising money for disaster relief. It seemed like every time I turned on the television, there was footage of him hugging someone else. Writer Lars Anderson, who wrote an eight-page cover story in *Sports Illustrated* about the football program's response to the storm, said in an interview that he would guess Coach Saban "hugged more people than anyone ever has in the history of this state" that summer. Though I had not yet met Coach Saban, it was encouraging to know I was playing for a man who had a mindset that stretched far beyond the game of football.

As a walk-on freshman, it took me a while to feel as if I was a part of the community, but the stories I heard about the tornado that summer still hit home. For example, our teammate Carson Tinker had lost his girlfriend, Ashley Harrison, to the tornado. It took a while for Carson to rejoin the team because the tornado had flung him into a field one hundred yards away, resulting in a concussion, broken wrist, and a gash on his ankle. I hated to think about the hell he was going through at that time, mourning the loss of his girlfriend.

I think that seeing the community suffering so badly made us want to work harder and push ourselves more in practice. As the summer unfolded, there was an underlying understanding that football might be able to help bring hope to the city again. Coach Saban was quoted in a news article as saying, "We can create a psychological escape for the people of this town."

Just as football was an escape for me when I lost my brother—an avenue that brought me meaning and joy on the road to healing—maybe it could be the same for a football-saturated community like Tuscaloosa.

I couldn't tell if practice was so intense that summer because our coaches wanted us to win for the community or if that was just the way Alabama football was. I would find out that such intensity and perfection was the status quo at Alabama.

One of the craziest practices I remember that summer was when we ran two dozen consecutive 110-yard sprints with minimal breaks in between. It was brutal.

Before we began each sprint, all the strength coaches would yell, "Hands behind the line! Hands behind the line!" Those four words became so embedded in our brains. It was about doing all the little things right, like not jumping offsides.

At one point, a player accidentally jumped off the line before Coach Cochran told us to go.

"That's a penalty! Add another one!" Coach boomed.

Another time, Coach Cochran called out a player because he didn't think he was sprinting as hard as he could.

"Add another one!" he belted.

This happened multiple times. It was insane. Again, just how he liked it.

It didn't matter how hard most of us were running; it was about our performance *as a team*, as a collective unit. Just as the whole team would be penalized during a game if a player jumped offsides, Coach Cochran penalized all of us if someone didn't do *exactly* what was expected. He demanded perfection, and if we weren't perfect, then we all paid the price.

As important as it was to be in top-notch physical condition at Alabama, what was even more important was a player's mental condition—his ability to push himself when his body and mind were telling him to quit. Coach Cochran was a mental guru, and one of the things he would frequently say to us in the middle of practice was, "It's only pain!" This was another phrase that became ingrained in us.

During our morning or evenings runs, we'd hear him say, "It's only pain!" While sprinting up and down the steps at Bryant-Denny on Fridays—"It's only pain!" While maxing out on the bench press or squats or anything else in the weight room—"It's only pain!"

I've applied this phrase not only to football but also to other aspects of my life. One thing I like about the phrase is that it acknowledges that pain is there. When Coach Cochran would yell, "It's only pain!", he was not telling us that pain didn't exist or that we should ignore it. He recognized that the pain was real and that it hurts.

I think this is a crucial element to dealing with pain on any level, not just in football. In my own life, whenever adversity comes my way, I am sometimes tempted to ignore that the pain is there. That's because if I ignore its existence, sometimes it doesn't hurt as bad. The drawback is that if we ignore the pain in our lives, we never appropriately deal with it the way we need to. Although this might seem easier at first, it results in all kinds of long-term issues that mask the wounds we are hiding.

It's interesting that Coach Cochran usually yelled his phrase in an effort to push us harder. He wouldn't yell, "It's only pain!" and tell us to sit down and rest. Rather, he would yell, "It's only pain!" to motivate us to run faster or get one more repetition in—to push ourselves to the limit. In short, we would actually be pulled *deeper* into the pain we were already experiencing. But it was worth it in the end because we got through it. If I would have stopped running every time I felt an inkling of pain while running those 110-yard sprints, I'm convinced we'd still be out there running today . . . or he would have kicked me off the team.

Quitting is not a healthy way to deal with pain, nor is ignoring that it's there. But when you recognize the pain and deal with it, in football and in life, then you end up stronger because you've dealt with the pain at its deepest levels.

What I like most about the phrase is its hopeful element. "It's only pain" also implies a number of encouraging things: one, that pain is normal; two, that it has no foothold; and three, that it is temporary.

Pain is a normal thing; therefore we do not need to be surprised when it shows up in our lives. At Alabama, no one signed a letter of intent expecting the journey to be easy. It would have been ignorant to think that playing in one of the top football programs in the nation wouldn't involve any pain. Alabama is great year after year because of guys like Coach Cochran, who push his players to the limit, day after day.

It is the same for everything else in this life. We cannot expect life to always unfold smoothly. Ever since sin entered this world, everything we experience is fallen—from weather to relationships to sickness to death. It's more normal to experience pain than it is to experience no pain at all. The question is not whether or not pain will strike, because it will. The question is how we will deal with it when it comes.

Second, pain has no foothold. Coach Cochran used the word "only" for a reason—pain is only a feeling. Our pain did not define us. It did not have to affect us. No matter how bad we felt and no matter how strongly our minds and bodies told us to quit, we had a choice as to whether or not to listen to what our minds and bodies said. What was more important, succumbing to the pain we felt or elevating the betterment of the team above the cramps in our sides and aches in our legs?

In dealing with the loss of my brother, I was encouraged to know that the pain in my life did not define me. It had no foothold in who I was or who I wanted to become. Sure, it was a crucial part of my story, but it did not have to affect the way I treated people, it did not have to be a crutch for me as I ventured through life, and it did not have to turn me into a victim. I was blessed to have known Trent for the years that he was here.

Lastly, pain is temporary. Again, Coach Cochran used the word "only" because he knew that whatever we were feeling would eventually pass. Not only would it pass, but our willingness to push through it would benefit us and our team down the road.

When I lost my brother, I learned for the first time how real pain is and how badly it hurt. Honestly, I still have some days where it's as real as it was on April 1, 2007, and it hurts just as badly. But I'm always comforted by the reminder that my pain is only temporary. I hate that horrible things happen, but I'm thankful that my hope isn't in this world. (That would be a very depressing reality.) Dealing with the loss of a brother may be a cross that I carry the remainder of my life, just like the Tuscaloosa families who lost loved ones during the tornado, but one of these days, I'll leave this broken world behind and be reunited in heaven with Trent and more importantly with Jesus. My sufferings on this earth will be a small blip on the radar compared to the light and perfection of eternity.

17
Discipline and Disappointment

"There are two paths people can take. They can either play now and pay later, or pay now and play later. Regardless of the choice, one thing is certain. Life will demand a payment."
~John Maxwell, motivational speaker and author

"There are two pains in life. There is the pain of discipline and the pain of disappointment. If you can handle the pain of discipline, then you'll never have to deal with the pain of disappointment."
~Nick Saban, University of Alabama head football coach

By August, Coach Saban was finally permitted to join us at practice according to NCAA regulations. He joined the Crimson Tide for team camp the first week of August, but because I was not on the game day roster, I did not take part in team camp. Being unable to attend was a little disappointing, but a lot of freshmen have to work their way up the ladder, especially those who are walk-ons. So instead I got a two-week vacation, which wasn't all that bad either.

My first practice with Coach Saban was actually the week heading into our first game of the season against Kent State. Unfortunately, one of my first personal interactions with Coach Saban was something I wish had never happened.

It was one of my first practices in pads, and we were practicing in our indoor facility, which we did once a week. I was playing on the scout team defense against the first team offense on one half of the field, and Coach Saban was watching the first team defense play the scout team offense on the other half of the field.

At one point during our scrimmage, one of our star receivers caught a pass in my coverage area. Right when he caught it, I plunged into him while he was still in mid-air and flattened him. I immediately knew that I shouldn't have hit a starter that hard just a few days away from our first game of the year, but I had reacted on instinct because I was playing as hard as I could. I was trying to earn a spot. The unnamed receiver was okay (though he might have barked a few words at me), and he quickly hopped up and walked back to the huddle for another play. However, there was someone who wasn't okay: Coach Saban.

Apparently he had seen the incident take place all the way across the practice field. To this day, I'm still shocked he saw what happened because Coach Saban, being a defensive-minded coach, usually had his back turned to us while he was watching the first-team defense. He had to have seen my hit out of the corner of his eye at just the right moment. Before I knew it, he had blown his whistle and was angrily marching over to our field with his eyes locked on #23—me.

Well, this isn't good, I thought.

In seconds, one of the greatest college football coaches of all time was right in front of me, his face so flushed with anger that it matched the crimson on my uniform.

"What in the world are you doing?!" he screamed, his voice echoing throughout the facility, getting everyone's attention.

"Just playing football, Coach," I responded.

"Stop trying to be a hero!" he wailed. "You hear me?!"

"Yes, sir," I said.

"Stop trying to be a hero!" he yelled again.

"Yes, sir," I replied.

And he walked away.

I was never one for first impressions.

Coach Saban was hard on us, and, like Coach Cochran, he often motivated us through yelling and screaming. But I can honestly say that the fiercest personal interaction I ever had with Coach Saban was that one, which was, strangely, one of our first interactions. This is funny to look back on, but at the time, I thought he was going to put me on his "bad list" and humiliate me the remainder of the season. He didn't, thank goodness. Maybe he appreciated my fire. Whatever the case, I knew he didn't appreciate me unleashing a big hit on one of his star players.

As I would soon find out, Coach Saban was as kind as they come. I wasn't stupid, either—never again would I slam into one of his star players before game day. Coach Saban was personable and caring, no matter if he was dealing with his star players, starters, bench players, the roster that suited up for games, the rest of the roster, or the athletic trainer students who brought us water. I'd imagine it was difficult for someone who already had so much on his plate to have a personal relationship with all 130 players on the team, but he truly made an effort to personally know each and every one of us, no matter what our role on the team. This speaks volumes about who he is. As much as he wanted to win, he didn't use his players' football abilities to help him shine; he genuinely cared about the entire team. That was always his and Coach Cochran's main priority—to help us develop into men who would be successful when football was over. Like Coach Cochran, Coach Saban also pushed us extremely hard. That's the Alabama way.

Just as Coach Cochran would often say, "It's only pain!", Coach Saban often told us in practice, "You either suffer the pain of discipline now or the pain of disappointment later!" I feel like he said that phrase every day.

Coach Saban said this because if we didn't experience pain through disciplining ourselves in football—whether it was our work ethic, nutrition, or off-the-field choices—then there was a better chance of experiencing a more devastating pain later on, say after we had lost a must-win SEC game or a national championship game. Either way, pain was involved. It'd obviously be more rewarding to suffer the pain of discipline for seven months and win a national championship than to suffer the pain of disappointment and never even get there. Coach Saban was essentially saying that our success would be determined by how willing we were to suffer the pain of discipline in every facet of football, each and every day.

You either suffer the pain of discipline now or the pain of disappointment later.

It's no secret that I identify with concepts that involve pain. I think this is because pain is something I'm familiar with, and pushing through pain is sometimes a very difficult thing. In high school, the pain was more emotional and spiritual. At Alabama, it was more physical and mental. It was pain nonetheless—pain that required perseverance, resilience, and discipline to get through.

Pain, as Coach Saban teaches, is an opportunity—an opportunity to suffer for a greater good. If each player dedicated himself to suffering the pain of discipline during the season, then we had a better chance of achieving something great as a team.

The pain of discipline is not easy in any avenue of life. It's not always easy to do the right thing—to say no to daily temptations, whether they are sexual or social or whatever else. But this is why God has given us commandments and guidelines—not to control us, but to help us live our lives to the full (John 10:10: "I have come that they may have life, and have it to the full"). This helps guide us from experiencing the pain of disappointment later. The pain of discipline, in the Christian tradition, is an opportunity to "participate in the sufferings of Christ, so that you may be overjoyed when his glory is revealed," as the apostle Peter says in 1 Peter 4:13. The pain of discipline is an opportunity to enjoy Christ more by denying ourselves and clinging to truth. Author and theologian John Piper puts it this way: "I know of no other way to triumph over sin long-term than by faith to die with Christ to our old seductions, that is, to gain a distaste for them because of a superior satisfaction in God." This makes the pain of discipline fulfilling and meaningful.

This is just another example of how the principles that Coach Saban and his staff implemented went far beyond the gridiron. Sure, they were paid to coach football, but the things they said could be taken into all areas of life. What I found most interesting is that one of the themes to everything that they taught us—whether it was Coach Cochran repeating, "It's only pain!" or Coach Saban saying, "You either suffer the pain of discipline now or the pain of disappointment later!"—was the element of pain.

Once the season began, we would find out which route of suffering we had chosen: the pain of discipline or the pain of disappointment. More importantly, I had to ask myself: Which route does my life reflect? Which does yours reflect?

18

Understood and Accepted

"Christ never intended to cover up the dark side of life, but rather to illuminate a path through it."
~Dan Allender, Christian therapist and author

"The great spiritual call of the Beloved Children of God is to pull their brokenness away from the shadow of the curse and put it under the light of the blessing."
~Henri Nouwen, Dutch theologian, author, and priest

Being in Tuscaloosa that summer felt right. But it also took a while for Tuscaloosa to feel like home, and I'm not so sure it did as we headed into the regular season.

I think this was because, although friendships with teammates formed as we went through conditioning in June, July, and August, I longed to be known and understood on a deeper level. I might not have realized this at the time, but looking back, it's pretty obvious to me that it was why I didn't feel completely comfortable at Alabama at first.

As we entered the regular season, the only person on the team who knew my story was Dustin. This wasn't the fault of my teammates. I could have shared my story with someone if I wanted to, but talking about past pain—and the pain that I was still sifting through—was not necessarily something that I felt like talking about. It was difficult for me to bring up.

My story, however, was such a large part of who I was that it felt weird that no one knew about it—especially since I'd come from Centreville, where everyone in the community seemed to know my story. Of course, it was never about people knowing my story; rather, it was about feeling understood and accepted. Our pasts are a part of who we are and what we become, and I was no different. I guess I just didn't realize how important it was at the time to talk about it.

This is not to say that I didn't feel connected at Alabama or that I didn't make friends. In addition to Dustin, I also developed great relationships with guys like freshmen defensive backs Jerrod Bierbower and Caleb Castille (who later went on to star in the 2015 movie *Woodlawn*), sophomore long snapper MK Taylor, sophomore linebacker Tyler Owens, and junior linebackers Matt Tinney and Joshua Dickerson. We had a great crew. Along with sweating and bleeding together during practice, we would also eat together, hang out after practice together, go to the spa in the football complex together—everything. I think we were able to bond over the fact that, when it came to the roster, we were outsiders looking in. We weren't scholarship players, but we were putting in the work and making sacrifices. We all had endeavors to make the team or break into the lineup.

I also developed great relationships with athletic trainers Jeff Allen and Ginger Gilmore. We'd see them every day, and they took such good care of us that we naturally got closer with them. I enjoyed connecting with them on a spiritual level as well.

Still, as close as I was with the fellow preferred walk-ons and trainers, it took me a while to share my story and for anyone to know me *that* well. If anyone stalked me long enough on social media, they might have figured out that I had lost my brother and was frequently speaking at different places about that experience, but as is always the case, being truly known takes place in relationship with others—when we truly go through life with one another, when we let down our guards, become vulnerable, and allow ourselves to be fully known, no matter how scary it might be.

Heading into the first game of the season, all the kind, amazing people at Alabama might have been my friends, but they were yet to become my family.

As the season began, Barrett Jones started up a weekly Bible study for any player or coach who wanted to attend. We met once a week in the media room where Coach Saban conducted all his press conferences.

It was a good study, and twenty people or so would usually show up. Barrett usually led everyone through a passage of Scripture; then he would unpack the verses, and we would discuss what the passage meant to us as individuals or as a team.

Heading into the third week of the season, after defeating Kent State and Penn State (I still was not on the game day roster), Barrett decided to do something a little different. After going through a passage of Scripture like usual, he opened up the floor for any of us to share our testimonies.

Considering we were already knee-deep into the season, I had decided that if an opportunity ever opened up for me to share my story, I would. I had been with the team for over twelve weeks, and I felt an internal nudge that it was time to let my teammates know me on a new level. Most importantly, I wanted them to know that I was approachable—that they could confide in me if they ever needed someone to talk to. That summer, we were all very aware of the pain in this life because we were surrounded by it each and every day in Tuscaloosa.

When Barrett opened up the floor, I paused a little and then forced myself to stand up. It was one thing to be a guest speaker at a local high school and share my story to motivate and inspire people; it was quite another thing to share my story with teammates, to be transparent and vulnerable with them so they could know me better and so I could connect with them on a deeper level. It's a beautiful, terrifying thing to allow oneself to be more fully known.

I told them about Trent and April, 1, 2007, and I shared with them the impact that "Never, Never Quit" had on me as I journeyed through high school—how I was encouraged to sell out to God and never give up on God, regardless of my circumstance. I tried to be as real with them as I possibly could.

I'm sure I rambled for about ten minutes or so. Sharing my story with some of my teammates—people with whom I'd been sweating beneath the summertime Alabama sun—was much more difficult than sharing my story with people I hardly knew. But there was also something comforting about it because I felt like I was letting them into my life, welcoming them into the dark places of my soul, where maybe they'd also be able to see the light of Christ shining through.

Once I shared my testimony, my relationship with my teammates dramatically changed. That's not to say that things were bad relationally before, but my relationships just got much deeper. They grew stronger. My teammates saw a totally different side of me—the weak, vulnerable side. Today, I might be doing a lot of motivational speaking to help strengthen people, but the irony is that people most identify with my weaknesses, and this, somehow, helps strengthen them. When we allow others to see our brokenness, it strengthens everyone—because brokenness touches on our humanity at its core.

Behind every jersey—every profession, every identity, every title—is a human being with real weaknesses, real brokenness, and real struggles. Behind all this is a story. Whether or not we realize it, we all have stories that we, in the deepest parts of our being, yearn to share so we can feel understood. There's always a temptation to hide the broken pieces of our life—whether it's a trial we've had to endure or a sin we are trying to conquer or insecurities that abound from either of these—but when we give into this temptation and put up facades, it is more difficult to feel understood and it's nearly impossible to bless others with our brokenness.

Later on during my time at Alabama, I picked up a job at a nearby health club. One of my coworkers was an older gentleman named Mr. Lee, who worked as a janitor at the club. I don't even know his first name. I always just called him Mr. Lee.

Mr. Lee and I had great conversations about a variety of things—whether it was Alabama football or work or spiritual things. Mr. Lee lived with his brother, and sometimes his brother wasn't around to help him with the bad rash he had on his back. Because he felt comfortable around me, he would sometimes ask me to help him care for his rash. This, of course, was a vulnerable thing for him to ask, but once I started doing it, he felt comfortable enough to share with me that he too had lost a brother.

I was able to share my own struggles with him in the grieving process. Our friendship, though we were several decades apart in age, strengthened and grew deeper—all over a bad rash and shared brokenness in loss. The thing is, I felt like Mr. Lee helped me more than I helped him. Those conversations with him blessed my heart.

Meeting someone in his or her brokenness, no matter what it might be, no matter what level of brokenness it might be, whether it's a bad rash or losing a brother, tends to leave both parties more encouraged, stronger, and more understood than before.

This is exactly how it felt when I shared my testimony the third week of the season during my freshman year at Alabama. I had opened up, and my teammates had heard me. I felt more understood because they had experienced the *real* me—for maybe the first time. They had heard the depths of my story and seen my brokenness—and maybe this was the first step to my teammates becoming family.

19
The Crimson Tide

"I run on the road, long before I dance under the lights."
~Muhammad Ali, heavyweight boxing champion

"You're Dixie's football pride,
Crimson Tide, Roll Tide, Roll Tide!!"
~University of Alabama fight song

Every Thursday after practice, the roster for the upcoming game was posted on a big tack board in the locker room. Those who were on the game day roster would also have a red Alabama duffel bag sitting on top of their locker with game day sweats or travel gear inside. I dreamt of the day that I would see my name on the roster and find a bag sitting on top of my locker. For those who were not on the game day roster like myself, the goal each week from an individual standpoint was to card a stellar week of practice in the hope of being able to suit up on Saturday.

As the season ensued, however, I got pretty accustomed to not seeing my name on the list. Eight games into the season, I was yet to dress for a game and watch it from the sidelines. Instead I watched away games on television and home games in the stands from the players' section—which, believe me, was far from a bad seat.

I wasn't surprised that I wasn't on the game day roster (I was a walk-on freshman after all, at the bottom of the totem pole), but I'd be lying if I said I wasn't disappointed. As competitive as I am, I really wanted to break into the roster. Considering I was playing on both sides of the ball in high school, basically being on the field at all times, it was a challenging transition to suddenly not compete during the games, let alone not even stand on the sidelines. I was working so hard, harder than I had ever worked before, but because of the caliber of players on the team, there was sometimes the feeling that I was hardly progressing.

141

For a walk-on, it can sometimes feel like all the effort is futile because of the lack of fruit. Each time I saw the roster on Thursdays after practice, I walked away from the bulletin board with a sinking feeling in my chest.

All that being said, I also learned a lot about myself. Your selfishness is challenged to its core when you're in a situation like that. When you give your all for the betterment of a group or someone else and there is a lack of fruit on a personal level, you find out how selfless or selfish you really are.

At the same time, it was okay to have individual goals—but I had to remember, again and again, what playing on the Crimson Tide was all about. It wasn't about me. It was about the team. The community of Tuscaloosa. Bama Nation. The reality was that it was shaping up to be an incredible year, whether I was on the game day roster or not. We were 8–0—ranked No. 2 in the country behind LSU—and football was proving to be something that breathed life into a broken, desolate city.

We adopted the mantra "T-Town, Never Down"—a phrase with the same principles as "Never, Never Quit"—and it was obvious that we were playing for something much bigger than ourselves, for this was the way of the Crimson Tide. I decided in my mind that I would fight off discouragement and negativity and continue to give my all for the betterment of the team and the community, whether I dressed for a single game that season or not.

After a bye in Week 9, we headed into our Week 10 game against LSU with an opportunity to seize the top slot in the nation—and to do it in front of our home crowd. Unfortunately, there were a number of missed opportunities on our end, and we fell to LSU 9–6 in overtime. The close loss was heartbreaking.

There was a general understanding on the team that we would have to win our remaining three games if we wanted to have a chance at playing in the BCS National Championship.

The Crimson Tide won their Week 11 game on the road against Mississippi State and headed into Week 12—Senior Day—against Georgia Southern with one last opportunity to play in front of its home crowd before the final game of the regular season on the road against Auburn. Then there was the bowl game, but no one knew which bowl we'd end up in.

Leading into our game against Mississippi State, I felt like I had carded one of my best weeks of practice yet. The coaches had been playing me on the scout special teams kickoff unit, and I think that lining up for kickoffs in practice might have allowed me to showcase my speed in a different way. I felt that the coaches could see, maybe for the first time, how explosive I could be with an open field in front of me. That was why they had recruited me to begin with—because of my speed.

After practice on Thursday, I routinely checked the tack board in the locker and was jolted when I saw my name on the roster to dress on Saturday. I must say that I was very surprised. I had pretty much accepted in my mind that I would go the entire season without dressing for a regular season game. Was I looking at what I thought I was looking at? Did I misread something? Was there a mistake?

I checked again. Then again. And a final time. But there it was, not going away, listed beneath "Defensive Backs":

Taylor Morton, #23.

Next, I went to the locker room and saw a duffel bag sitting on the shelf of my locker. I stood there for a few seconds, trying to take it all in. On a personal level, the whole moment seemed surreal. Surviving training camp and being on the team was one thing, but thinking about slipping on an Alabama game day jersey and running through the tunnel at Bryant-Denny in front of 102,000 fans was quite another. I had made it. As a freshman. As a walk-on.

I understand this might sound like a small feat for some, but for me it was a momentous step in the right direction. I wanted to help the team any way I could and as much as I possibly could. Being on the game day roster, in my mind, was another way to help the team. Coach Cochran always told us that it was the players' jobs on the sidelines to be motivators and encouragers—to keep the sidelines alive because those on the field would be able to feed off of this energy. I couldn't wait for Saturday.

I guess the only thing I was nervous about was tripping when I ran out onto the field.

+++

On Saturday afternoon, I walked from my dorm over to the stadium in my Alabama football sweats. Our game wasn't until six thirty that evening, but we were expected to get there two hours early. The campus was already hopping.

A couple hours before the game, we got dressed in the locker room, and I slipped on my crimson game day jersey for the first time.

While stretching in the locker room before taking the field for warm-ups, seventy minutes before the game, you could hear coaches yelling, "Hands behind the line! Hands behind the line!" As you might remember, this was what they yelled during our 110-yard sprints in summer conditioning. By repeating the phrase before the game, it was as if they were subtly reminding us of all our hard work and that we were prepared—we had suffered the pain of discipline.

After warm-ups, we returned to the locker room, and all the players met with their defensive or offensive coach. Then Coach Saban said a few words to the entire team, and before walking through the tunnel and taking the field, all the players and coaches gathered around, joined hands, and recited the Lord's Prayer.

Our Father in heaven,
Hallowed be Your name.
Your kingdom come,
Your will be done,
On earth, as it is in heaven.
Give us this day our daily bread,
And forgive us our debts,
As we also have forgiven our debtors.
And lead us not into temptation,
But deliver us from evil.

After the prayer, we huddled up, and then we headed toward the tunnel. Marching to the tunnel, you could hear the shuffling of our legs and the continuous *pat-pat* of players' cleats on the concrete. We were like an army, our movements echoing through the halls as the roar of the crowd grew progressively louder and the intro to AC/DC's "Thunderstruck" played throughout the stadium. As tradition goes, we all touched a hanging white PVC pipe that had "WIN" painted on it in red, and then we rubbed the head of a Bear Bryant statue before stepping into the tunnel.

Walking through the tunnel, the decibel level reached its peak. No longer was the noise bleeding through the walls or navigating its way through hallways; no longer was it muffled; now it was coming directly from the source, blasting its way down the tunnel. It was the loudest thing I had ever heard in my life—102,000 fans yelling and screaming, waiting for their team to emerge.

And then it was time to do just that.

We walked out of the tunnel, led by Coach Saban, went past the field goal post, and came to a halt in the north end zone. It felt like we were gladiators walking into the Colosseum. All I saw was a sea of crimson and white flowing seemingly endlessly into the sky.

Once the fans saw the players appear in the end zone, Bryant-Denny somehow grew even louder. Then, once we started to run up the center of the field, led by members of the cheer squad carrying three gigantic Alabama flags, with the marching band and cheerleaders lining both sides of our path, the crowd exploded into pandemonium. After so much build up, it was as if someone pressed a button to launch a rocket.

Don't trip, don't trip, don't trip, I kept thinking to myself as I ran. I didn't, thank goodness. I would have hated to forever live in infamy on the Internet.

The first time running onto the field at Bryant-Denny was unforgettable, but the truth is that I could do it a thousand times and get chills each time. It was a moment that I had dreamt about since I was a kid, ever since I had sat in our family seats next to the tunnel and had seen Will Oakley, #7, walk beneath us and then run up the center of the field as the crowd went wild. I always wanted to be like Will Oakley, to wear that Alabama uniform on Saturdays in Tuscaloosa, and to take the field in front of thousands of screaming fans. Finally, after all those years, my time had finally come.

We defeated Georgia Southern 45–21. For most of the players on the team, that blowout game might not have been something worth writing about, but for me, it was a day that I will never forget—my first experience with the Tide on game day.

Following the game, I got my first taste of what a winning locker room was like at the University of Alabama. Once we were all in the locker room, after some of the players' and coaches' media appearances, Coach Saban gathered everyone together, congratulated us, and said a few brief things about the game. Then we bowed our heads, held hands, and recited the Lord's Prayer together once again.

I'm not sure when Alabama players started saying the Lord's Prayer in the locker room—I assume it's been a longstanding tradition—but I found it to be something that provided great perspective for all of us, especially considering all the emotions players and coaches experience during an SEC college football game. When thousands of people treat you like a god just because you're wearing an Alabama jersey, there is sometimes the temptation to believe that you are more special or important than you really are. Saying the Lord's Prayer, no matter each individual's beliefs, seemed to be a reminder that there were bigger things than football. After all, if the beginning and end of our identities lay in a silly game with a pigskin, we would inevitably be let down later in life.

For me as a believer, saying the Lord's Prayer was a reminder of why I played the game in the first place and why I lived the way I did—to enjoy Him and glorify Him in everything that I did, work or play. I would later learn that we prayed this prayer in the locker room no matter the game's outcome, win or lose. Honoring God was something that was worth way more than any trophy or accolade.

After saying the Lord's Prayer, we then sang "Yea Alabama" as a team, the Crimson Tide fight song that has been around since the 1920s:

Yea, Alabama!
Drown 'em Tide!
Every Bama man's behind you,
Hit your stride.
Go teach the Bulldogs to behave,
Send the Yellow Jackets to a watery grave.
And if a man starts to weaken,
That's a shame!

For Bama's pluck and grit have
Writ her name in Crimson flame.
Fight on, fight on, fight on men!
Remember the Rose Bowl, we'll win then.
Go, roll to victory,
Hit your stride,
You're Dixie's football pride,
Crimson Tide, Roll Tide, Roll Tide!!

Following the conclusion of the song, we counted, in unison, up to the number of points we scored. In our 45–21 victory over Georgia Southern, we counted from one to forty-five. This was our final hoorah before winding down and changing out of our gear.

As we settled down, Coach Saban made his way around the locker room and shook hands with each individual player, including those who hadn't played. He always told us, "It takes a team of individuals doing their job, no matter what it is."

After getting changed, I met up with family and friends outside Gate 47, next to our locker room. Included in this group were two close family friends, Kenny Murphy (my former Little League baseball coach) and David Steele (a softball coach at West Blocton). I also remember signing my first autograph for a young boy outside Gate 47. I'm sure the little kid asking for my autograph had no idea who I was or that I hadn't played, but considering the type of year we were having, all that mattered to him was that I played for the Crimson Tide.

I wanted to tell the poor kid that my signature on his football made it worth a lot less money, but it also took me back to when I was a kid. Anyone on the field, whether I knew who they were or not, was a star—because they were a part of the Crimson Tide. Whether you were A.J. McCarron or the water boy, you were a part of Alabama football. And the coaches expected anyone who wore crimson and white to be a role model—to conduct himself in a way that any kid can emulate.

It was a reminder to me that all of us are role models in some way to someone. Speaker and author Brent Crowe says in his book *Chasing Elephants*, "This is the great challenge for us today . . . to live lives worthy of imitation. Fewer ideas are more convicting and motivating than the thought that someone could be imitating us, following us as an example. Yet, this is the goal of freedom: that in following our example, others will be led to the feet of Jesus."

It doesn't matter if you are setting an example for one person or a million people because one of the most valuable things we can do in this life is impact someone for the better. Playing for the Crimson Tide was a tremendous blessing because of the platform it gave me to impact people.

Because of this reality, I started signing as many autographs as I possibly could whenever I had the opportunity. Next to my signature, I would write "Philippians 3:14" and "Never, Never Quit," two things that encapsulate my story and my drive. At first glance, people always think it's Philippians 4:13 ("I can do all things through Christ who strengthens me") because that's such a commonly quoted verse, especially by athletes, but I wanted to challenge people to look up Philippians 3:14.

More than anything, I saw signing an autograph as an opportunity to impact kids and maybe make their day. Who knows? Maybe it'd be something they'd always remember, just as I always remembered my interactions with Will Oakley.

I was beginning to see that playing for Alabama was giving me a unique platform. For now, maybe it was just an autograph. But in the future, maybe it'd be my story.

I didn't dress for our final game of the regular season against Auburn. Whereas 115 players or so dress for home games, usually no more than 85 dress for away games during the regular season. I had a long way to go if I wanted to travel with the team.

We defeated Auburn, our rival, to finish the regular season with a 12–1 record, our only loss coming against LSU in our ninth game of the season. Thanks to our regular season dominance, beating each of our opponents by 16 points or more, we were still awarded the No. 2 slot in the BCS National Championship against, yes, the No. 1 team in the country, LSU—a fitting rematch. Pundits began calling it "The Game of the Century."

Although the coaches only allowed a certain number of players to dress in the regular season games, every player was asked to travel to New Orleans and dress for the national championship. This fed into the coaches' philosophy that no player was more important than any other player and that each and every player who was with the team at the end of the season deserved to reap the benefits. Each player was a valuable asset to the team—the coaches really believed that. Though I've heard a number of stories from walk-ons at other schools about how they sometimes felt unequal or as if they weren't part of the team, there was none of that at Alabama. Each player was equal. No matter his role.

Though our first matchup against LSU was at Bryant-Denny, our rematch against them in the national championship game was just an hour and a half away from their home field in Baton Rouge—in New Orleans, Louisiana.

20
Back to Louisiana

*"Our greatest fear should not be of failure, but of succeeding
at something that doesn't really matter."*
~Anonymous

The last trip that Trent went on before he passed away was when he and my dad took a road trip to Baton Rouge in mid-November 2006 to watch Alabama play LSU at Tiger Stadium, known as Death Valley. Trent was a seventh grader at Bibb County Junior High, and a lady named Avis Huey, who worked in the school office, had two tickets for the game in Baton Rouge. She knew Trent loved LSU, and she loved Trent, so she offered them to my dad. When Dad bought them and informed Trent that they were going to the Alabama/LSU game in November, my brother couldn't have been more excited, and he began counting down the days.

Dad and Trent left early the day of the game, but when they pulled over at a rest stop in Meridian, Mississippi, Dad somehow sprained his ankle pretty severely while walking to the bathroom. Trent hated seeing Dad hurt and said to him, "Daddy, if you do not feel like going, we can go home."

But there was no way Dad was going to drive them back to Centreville considering how much Trent loved LSU. Dad could have broken his leg, but he somehow would have still gotten them to Baton Rouge.

They arrived in Baton Rouge about four hours before kickoff and walked around the campus. (Well, Dad hobbled as Trent absorbed everything like a sponge.) Dad took several pictures of Trent around campus, and today, those are some of our fondest snapshots of Trent. Our favorite is one that Dad took of Trent wearing his #4 LSU JaMarcus Russell jersey and a purple and gold LSU hat and standing next to an American flag on the quad an hour or so before the game, with the

Louisiana sun setting behind him. It's a beautiful picture, and Trent is glowing with joy.

Dad, of course, was decked out in Alabama gear. When he and Trent ran into some friends from Bibb County at the game, they gave Dad a hard time for letting his son wear LSU garb. But Trent loved his Tigers.

The two of them sat in the upper deck of a sold-out Tiger Stadium beneath the lights of a Saturday evening game—Dad says it's one of those classic "father and son moments" that he'll always remember. Also, Dad was the only one in their section wearing Alabama gear. LSU fans were literally all around him. Maybe it was an opportunity for Dad to embarrass Trent after Trent had embarrassed him for liking LSU all those years.

All in all, LSU ended up winning the game 28–14. Dad and Trent headed back north after the game and spent the night in Jackson, Mississippi. All the way back to Alabama, Trent kept saying over and over, "Daddy, that's the best time I've ever had."

When Trent died six months later, Carla Hubbard—the mother of Trent's best friend Kendal—reached out to the athletic department at LSU and informed them of our situation and how much Trent loved the Tigers. Trent loved Carla and spent a lot of time at their home. He was like another son to her.

A few weeks later, my family received a letter that had been personally written by Les Miles, the head coach at LSU. The letter said:

May 24, 2007

Dear Terry and Tammy,

I recently received an email from Carla Hubbard telling me about the loss of your son Trent in a four-wheeler accident. My heart goes out to your family. I have four children of my own and cannot imagine the pain you must be going through. The email mentioned that Trent was a devoted TIGER FAN! I would have loved to have met Trent. I know he was a special young man and that he will be greatly missed by all.

My thoughts and prayers are with you and your family.

Sincerely,

Les Miles
Head Football Coach

It was honestly kind of shocking to receive something from Coach Miles. People of that status get thousands of emails a year about all kinds of things, so to think that he and the thoughtful people at LSU took the time to reach out to us was very encouraging. Any type of support that we received was comforting, but getting a letter from the head coach of LSU made us feel like Trent's legacy was continuing to be preserved, that his story was getting out there, and that people, on all levels, from every stage of life, from every social status, were truly caring about what we were going through.

My parents wrote Coach Miles back and included some pictures of Trent in his LSU gear. They also mentioned that they would be at the LSU/Alabama game in late October. Coach Miles wrote them back once more:

October 23, 2007

Dear Mr. and Mrs. Morton,

Thank you for your note and kind words. Thank you for the pictures of Trent as well. I am happy to hear that you will be attending next week's game. We continue to keep your family in our thoughts and prayers. The Tigers and I are excited about the season and hope to continue our success. Your thoughtfulness and kindness are truly appreciated. Geaux Tigers!

Sincerely,

Les Miles
Head Football Coach

Now, five years later, I was going back to Louisiana, where Trent had one of the best trips of his life, to play for Alabama against LSU, Trent's favorite team—in the BCS National Championship.

As a player, I had six tickets for family members, and I could not help but think about how excited Trent would have been for another Alabama and LSU showdown and how much he would have enjoyed attending the game, just like five years before.

After our last game of the season against Auburn in late November, we had more than a month to prepare for the BCS National Championship on January 9, 2012 (this was before the current NCAA playoff system was established). It was weird having so much time to prepare for a single game, but the coaches took full advantage of the situation.

Coach Saban told us that we were going to "prepare for a one-game season," so we went through a miniature conditioning program and even went through a miniature team camp. The coaches, as always, pushed us to our limits. There was no coasting. We were working as hard as we had ever worked, and in many ways, it still felt like we were right in the middle of the season—because there was nothing in our workouts or the things our coaches were saying to us that indicated that our season was winding down. It really was as if we were preparing for a one-game season.

Then, one week before the national championship game against LSU, the entire Alabama roster boarded two Delta jet planes to fly down to New Orleans, Louisiana—my first time traveling with the team. A year before, I thought playing for Alabama was completely out of the question, and now I was on a plane to New Orleans for the national championship.

It was all business, though. That's how Coach Saban approached every away game. He would even tell the team, "It's a business trip." And we had seven days of practice down in New Orleans to prepare ourselves to finish the deal—to redeem ourselves after losing to LSU in the regular season and bring home Alabama's fourteenth national championship.

Throughout the week, we were with one another 24/7. Each day was filled with team activities and preparation. We practiced at nearby colleges as well as at the Superdome, home of the New Orleans Saints, where the game would be held on Monday evening. I knew I wasn't going to play, but my goal was the same as it had been all season: play my hardest on the scout team defense so as to challenge the first-team offense. Considering the defensive showdown between LSU and us during the regular season, there was a chance that offense might be the deciding factor in the game.

As Coach Saban said, going to New Orleans wasn't a vacation; it was a business trip. We had a strict practice schedule and a strict curfew. Everything revolved around one goal—a goal that we had been trying to achieve together since summer conditioning, a goal we had been trying to achieve for the community since a tornado bulldozed its way through Tuscaloosa.

Six of my family members were in attendance at the BCS National Championship: Mom, Dad, T.J., Nana, my Aunt Sue, and Pate Oakley, who isn't biologically a family member but is an Oakley so is pretty much my family member.

Though we were in LSU's home state, our fans traveled well, and the 78,000 in attendance at the Superdome seemed pretty divided—crimson and white on one side, purple and gold on the opposite side. It looked spectacular. And throughout the game, the Superdome was as loud as it could be. With nowhere for the noise to escape, it was deafening in there when the fans got rowdy.

These eruptions were mostly because of our defense.

LSU didn't even cross midfield into Bama territory until there were only eight minutes left in the game. Overall, their offense only totaled 92 yards, five first downs, and no touchdowns or field goals. Our defensive shutout was the first in the fourteen-year history of the BCS, and some in the media wrote that our defense that season was the best in college football history, all climaxing in the national championship game. It was old-school football at its finest.

As the game clock ticked down to its final seconds, it was obvious we were going to win (we were up 21–0, with five field goals and a late-game touchdown with a missed PAT), and the celebration officially began.

Everything happened so fast, and it was all so surreal, but I remember me, Jerrod Bierbower, Levi Cook, Aaron Joiner, and Dustin Ellison all looking at each other as crimson and white confetti fell from the roof of the Superdome. No words needed to be said. It was as if we all realized that this was what we had worked so hard for all year. This was why we got up at four thirty in the morning for a five o'clock workout and then went to class, why we slept four hours a night, why we ate properly, why we ran to the point of puking, why we got one more rep in when our legs or arms were numb and tingly, and why we dedicated our lives to representing Crimson Tide football and making the program better. For a moment like this.

Roll Tide.

Coach Saban had said at the start of the season that the game of football presented an opportunity to be a psychological escape for the good people of Tuscaloosa who were affected by the tornado, and this was exactly what happened, all reaching its crescendo in that moment in New Orleans.

Winning a national championship—holding the crystal football as confetti fell and fireworks went off, throwing our arms around one another, and celebrating with our beloved fans—was an indescribable feeling. It all felt larger-than-life. It was difficult to digest and even more difficult to explain. Other than yelling "Roll Tide!" multiple times during the celebration, I'm not sure I said much at all. Nothing needed to be said. It was pure elation. Total euphoria. Pure adrenaline.

When quarterback A.J. McCarron, the national championship offensive MVP, was interviewed after the game, the first thing he said was, "I first want to thank the scout team defense; our offense wouldn't be as good without them." Not only was that a kind gesture that meant a lot to all of us on the scout team; it was also the Alabama way—a daily mindset emphasizing every moment with each player's role, no matter what it was.

When we finally got back to the locker room, we said the Lord's Prayer and sang "Yea Alabama," like usual. Singing "Yea Alabama" was always enjoyable, but there was something especially full about singing it there in New Orleans.

Next, Coach Saban said to us, "You have tonight to celebrate in New Orleans and tomorrow to celebrate in Tuscaloosa. After that, all those who are returning will meet up to talk about next season."

Of course, celebrating also meant that, for the first time all week, we didn't have a curfew—only a flight to board at five-thirty the next morning.

The first thing we did after the game was go back to our hotel, the New Orleans Marriott, which was only a four-minute walk from Bourbon Street. I wasn't able to meet up with my family, but I texted all of them right after the game. As our buses pulled up, a mob of Alabama fans crowded around, and we had to be escorted by state troopers back to our rooms. The hoopla was absolutely insane, unlike anything I had ever felt before.

I was rooming with a junior defensive back named Diege Barry all week, so we went back to our room and changed into our Alabama sweats. When we came back down to the lobby, our fans were still there, anxiously waiting for us. We no longer had security guards and state troopers escorting us, so it really was a mob. And I don't think anyone cared. We wanted to be with our fans.

That night, I probably signed over one hundred autographs. I can't imagine how many autographs guys like A.J. or Eddie signed. I even had one fan on Bourbon Street offer me four hundred dollars for my gray snapback national championship hat that said "DONE" in bolded letters followed by "2011 NATIONAL CHAMPIONS" below. Of course I said no—first and foremost because that would have been an NCAA violation, but also because I wouldn't have sold that hat for anything. (Now, however, you can buy one of those hats for about four dollars on Amazon.)

I tried to approach each moment that evening, every autograph and conversation, as an opportunity to glorify God. All of a sudden I had a natural opportunity to share what I believed on the largest stage in college sports, and I didn't know if I'd ever have an opportunity like that again.

Most of us didn't get back to the hotel until about four thirty in the morning, which only gave us an hour to get packed up and ready to board our flight. Considering we had been in New Orleans for an entire week, my clothes were scattered all over the floor and bathroom, and it took me a while to get my belongings together. I made it, though. All of us did.

Overall, it was an unforgettable experience. It was also eye-opening on a number of levels. Some of the guys might have been somewhat used to the fame that comes with playing for the University of Alabama, but for most of us walk-ons, this was our first time experiencing hoopla to the point that we couldn't even walk down the street without being asked to sign something or take a picture with someone.

At the same time, experiencing all this was a reminder to anchor my life in things that really last. At the end of the day, the hype always wears off, the stardom always fades, and the trophies and rings no longer glimmer like they once did. All of it is temporary. Exciting, yes. But it'd be a foolish thing to anchor my life in the things of this world, because all these things, as mesmerizing as they may be, as glamorous as they may seem, always pass, always fade, always become meaningless in the grand scheme of eternity.

I was reminded that the only thing that really lasts is a relationship with Christ; this is something we can enjoy forever. In Him, we experience life to the full here on earth, even if it's hard, and we get to enjoy Him throughout eternity. Death was in the world, even on the mountaintops, but true life was found in living for Christ and asking Him to live through me.

21
The Purple Balloon

"So the Tide showed us what it takes to win as a team, but they also showed what it means to be a part of a larger community: to look out for one another, to help. And that makes them pretty special."
~Barack Obama, 44th President of the United States

When Coach Saban told us after winning the national championship that we had forty-eight hours to celebrate before we got back to work again, he wasn't kidding. Throughout January and the first two weeks of February, we lifted weights. By mid-February, we began the "Fourth Quarter Program," which continued throughout the month of March.

If I had to describe the Fourth Quarter Program, I would describe it as this: a living hell. The purpose of the program was to dive into the intensity of Alabama football conditioning once more—with a focus on cardiovascular conditioning, strength, endurance, and mental toughness. During the season, practices and workouts were more strategic in order to prevent injuries and make sure we had plenty of energy on game day. During the spring and summer, however, it was all about conditioning and pushing our bodies to their limits. The Fourth Quarter Program was the beginning of this. And it was brutal.

Without going into too much detail, one of the staples of the Fourth Quarter Program was running 110s, which focused on bursts and recovery. We sprinted as fast as we could from one end of the field into the opposite end zone, had forty-five seconds of rest, and then did it again. Each player was required to run sixteen of these to pass one of Coach Cochran's many cardiovascular tests, and we were challenged to run more than sixteen. The thinking behind the sixteen 110s was running four per quarter, totaling sixteen; the goal was to increase our stamina so that our final four 110s could be run faster than those of any other opponent on any other team in the country. This was where games were won—in the fourth quarter; you had to have the strength and endurance to outlast your opponent.

Each player was also given a thick, 100-plus-page book detailing the program and its purpose. The book is filled with nutritional information, instruction for certain drills and tests, and fuel for the mindset and mental toughness of a true champion. One of my favorite quotes in the book was this one by legendary Alabama Coach Bear Bryant: "It's not the will to win that matters—everyone has that. It's the will to prepare to win that matters."

The Fourth Quarter Program not only set the tone for the season from a physical standpoint but also set the tone from a mental standpoint. We were challenged as players to ask some difficult questions about ourselves in order to spark personal growth and change. Sometimes when you are working really hard, you forget to self evaluate. It can also be easy to get frustrated about the lack of fruit from your labor—this was a struggle of mine, as you know. Coach Cochran would sometimes tell us: "Mental toughness is being able to create positive emotions upon command, enabling you to bring all your talent and skills to life in a moment." What a challenge! The real battle was in our minds, our thinking, and our daily approach.

We were also challenged to take delight in our role on the team, whatever it was—to choose sacrifice over selfishness. At Alabama, there were few things that were more important than the unity and oneness of the team.

The Fourth Quarter Program was grueling from a physical standpoint and introspective from a mental standpoint. As much as we might have dreaded the program at the time, it ingrained in our minds that our will to prepare, both physically and mentally, would be the difference between being good and great. Sure, we all loved the idea of winning a national championship. But our will to prepare, even seven months before the start of the season, would determine our success.

In late March of my freshman year, it dawned on me that my family and I were approaching the fifth-year anniversary of Trent's death. I couldn't believe it had been that long. And, at the same time, it sometimes felt like it happened yesterday.

Most people who know me would probably tell you that I'm not the most emotional person, and even when I am, I hardly express it, but as I approached April 1, 2012, it was as if the pain became real again, as real as it had been on April 1, 2007. As I've said before, the death of a family member becomes easier to handle as more time passes, but the weird thing is that it also resonates in new and different ways.

One day, I needed to talk to someone so I dropped by Coach Cochran's office and opened up to him about Trent and some of my struggles. He had an open-door policy with his players and always encouraged us that we could drop by and talk to him about anything. This meant the world to me. I left his office strengthened and encouraged.

Something about it being five years, half a decade, since the accident reminded me of all that had happened in my life in such a short time span—all the memories at Bibb County as Coach Battles led us to some of the most successful seasons in Choctaw football history and all the memories in one season at the University of Alabama, which included a national championship. This consequently reminded me that Trent had missed all of it. Don't get me wrong; I was very thankful for all the things I had been blessed with, particularly in the football realm; I only wished I could have also shared the memories with Trent.

Two weeks into April, the University of Alabama hosted its annual A-Day Spring Football Game. I had attended A-Day the year before as a high school senior to sign my letter of intent, but the 2012 A-Day was my first as a player. Needless to say, I was excited.

Since A-Day was an intrasquad game, just about everyone on the team was given some time on the field. This was an exciting thing for a walk-on freshman to think about. There was always such a buzz around campus on A-Day, and Bryant-Denny was always packed pretty full, as if it was a regular season game (admission was free). It would be my first time actually *playing* in front of our fans.

We had a few things riding on the game as players. The tradition at the University of Alabama is that the Crimson Team and White Team play each other for dinner that evening. The players on the losing team have to eat "beanie weenies"—baked beans and hot dogs on paper plates with plastic silverware—while the players on the winning team chow down on delicious steaks with fancy plates and silverware as waiters and waitresses bring them whatever they'd like, right in front of the losing team.

Most importantly, this particular A-Day was exciting because each of us would finally receive our national championship rings. It had been almost four months since winning it all in January, and since ample time had passed for us to digest what we had achieved, we were excited to get our individual bling—something that we would be able to show our children and grandchildren and keep forever in the lineage of our families.

During the A-Day game, I played safety and special teams and had a couple of tackles and a couple of deflected passes. I played a lot and played well, which got me even more excited for the season. I really felt that I was continuing to progress and climb within the ranks of our team. I knew I still had a ways to go, but I hoped my sophomore year might be a breakout year for me.

Though A-Day was really just a glorified practice, it was neat to play in front of the Crimson Tide fans. The coaches were as intense as usual, and, even though it was an intrasquad game, each moment and each play was taken just as seriously as a big-time SEC rivalry game. At Alabama, each moment as it related to football was treated as if it were dire. This made it easier to perform under pressure in, say, a national championship game—because we had conditioned our minds to take everything seriously and had replicated the seriousness of each play over and over in our minds, making it easier for our subconscious to take over when we were really in a high-pressure moment.

Unfortunately, I was on the losing team, so we didn't get the steak I was craving. Most thought the beanie weenies were gross, but I kind of liked them—they were better than anything I could have fixed up back at my apartment.

Though my team lost, things ended up working out all right. We scarfed down our beanie weenies and received our championship rings while the winning team enjoyed their steaks. We might have had stomachaches, but we also had our rings.

Five days later, we were given the opportunity of a lifetime—to meet President Barack Obama at the White House as he recognized us in front of the entire nation for winning a national championship. This was the final event associated with our championship season for us to really enjoy. After this trip, we understood that we'd be focusing headstrong on the 2012–13 season, starting all over, and leaving past successes far behind.

We woke up early on Thursday, April 19, for a six o'clock meeting with the head of football operations at the facility. He prepared us for the happenings of the day and explained that the White House would be running background checks on each of us.

Next, we hopped on charter buses to the Tuscaloosa Regional Airport, where we crammed onto a single plane for the two-hour flight to Washington D.C. We landed at Washington Dulles International Airport mid-morning, and a bus picked us up to take us straight to the White House.

It was crazy seeing the intricacy of the White House security's protocol as we got checked in. It made sense since we were meeting the President and all, but it was extravagant nonetheless. They knew our names, backgrounds—everything. It was kind of scary.

Eventually, we were escorted to the White House lawn. Coach Saban was escorted a different way. The first time we saw President Obama was moments later when he and Coach Saban walked toward us across the lawn.

It hardly seemed real. You are so used to seeing President Obama on television that when you see him in person, it feels like you're looking at a cartoon or something. It was Coach Saban's second time meeting President Obama. Or, as people in Alabama like to say, "It was President Obama's second time meeting Coach Saban."

President Obama delivered a great speech and honored our team not only for winning the national championship but also for the efforts of the players and coaches in the community of Tuscaloosa in the wake of the tornado. He concluded his speech in saying, "So the Tide showed us what it takes to win as a team, but they also showed what it means to be a part of a larger community: to look out for one another, to help. And that makes them pretty special."

Following President Obama's speech, which was televised across the country on ESPN, our captain, Barrett Jones, presented the President with a #14 Alabama jersey and a #14 Alabama helmet—since it was the Tide's fourteenth national championship. (They had won their thirteenth national title in 2009, which was Coach Saban's first with Alabama and the Tide's first since 1992, when I was born.) With it being an election year, President Obama said to us, "I'll probably need a helmet between now and November, what do ya think?"

After we presented him with the jersey and helmet and as the gathering came to a close, President Obama casually said, "Best of luck next season. Who knows? I may see you again."

He then went around and talked to each one of us.

Regardless of how you feel about President Obama's political views or ideals, I must say it was neat to shake hands with such a historical president, the first African-American president in our country's history. I'm not one to get star-struck, but I admit that I completely froze when I shook hands with him.

"Congratulations," he said to me.

"Congratulations," I responded.

He had to have been thinking to himself, *Why did this kid just congratulate me?*

That May, I went home for what would have been Trent's graduation ceremony, held at Bibb County's football field. The administration reserved an empty chair where Trent would have sat. Tied to the chair was a purple balloon. Trent's classmates initiated the remembrance of Trent during graduation, which was a nice reminder to all of us that his peers had not forgotten about him.

My parents didn't go to graduation because they didn't want to be a distraction. They didn't want to be crying in the stands and drawing attention to themselves, and they didn't want people to feel sorry for them. They didn't want to subtract anything from the families who were celebrating such a crowning accomplishment of their children's high school careers. Still, they visited the field with me and T.J. several hours before the start of the ceremony and before anyone else had arrived. I admit that it was eerie looking across the rows of gray chairs and seeing one purple balloon floating in the middle of it all.

During the ceremony, Bibb County High School presented a plaque to our family in memory of Trent, which T.J. and I accepted on stage while my parents watched the ceremony in the distance from a nearby hillside. Upon presenting the plaque to us, they also cut the string of the purple balloon and everyone silently watched it rise into the sky. My parents watched from the hillside as the balloon rose from the football field and eventually vanished in the distance.

22
Back-To-Back

"It is not what we get but who we become, what we contribute . . . that gives meaning to our lives."
~Tony Robbins, motivational speaker

"Only those who have learned the power of sincere and selfless contribution experience life's deepest joy: true fulfillment."
~Tony Robbins

In late May, it was once again time for spring training. It was hard to believe that I was already entering my sophomore season at Alabama. My personal goal was to dress for home and away games and to break into the playing roster. It seemed that it wasn't that long ago that Coach Cochran had said to me, "You better pick it up or you won't last long here." Well, I had lasted through one year at Alabama and was eager to begin my second.

There was nothing easier about Coach Cochran's two-a-day workouts this time around, and there was nothing cooler about the Alabama summer. Though we had received our rings and visited the White House in April, the month of May reminded us all that our 2011 national championship was long gone. We were starting over. And we all had one goal in mind: to not die during Coach Cochran's workouts.

Thankfully we had Aaron Joiner, a senior offensive lineman, to help lighten the mood. Aaron was a burly white guy who had a thick face and a scruffy beard. I think most of my former teammates would agree that he was the funniest guy on the team. Every day before practice, for example, while we did stretches as a team, he would call out each stretch in the most intense manner, yelling angrily and keeping a straight face while doing so. We were doing the simplest of things—stretching—but he treated it with the intensity of being down by one touchdown in the national championship game. And he did it all without laughing.

It always gave us a much-needed chuckle, because we all knew that once Coach Cochran emerged from his lair and stepped onto the field, we were doomed. We were like pigs that knew they would eventually be butchered. So we enjoyed the simple things in life like laughing at Aaron Joiner's jokes during stretches.

Throughout the summer, I began branching out more and more, and my brotherhood with my teammates grew even stronger. My freshman year I was sort of learning the ropes as everything was new, but it all seemed to click into place my sophomore year. I was starting to really establish myself as a player and a brother to my teammates after being there a full year. Many of my teammates even began coming to Converge events and my speaking engagements to support me. It was always neat to see relationships with teammates at Alabama go far beyond the football field.

On the field, the theme was the same. The coaches once again had me playing on special teams and on defense as a defensive back. I was fortunate to learn from guys like Ha Ha Clinton-Dix, a sophomore defensive back who went on to get drafted in the first round of the 2014 NFL Draft, and Vinnie Sunseri, another sophomore defensive back who went on to get drafted in the fifth round of the 2014 NFL Draft. Since I never played defensive back in high school, Ha Ha and Vinnie were instrumental in teaching me the nuances of the position and how to play it intelligently.

They taught me everything from the fundamentals to improving my footwork to understanding the different plays in a playbook. They were great players to learn from—two of the best college defensive backs in the country. It was easy to see that they were true leaders, the kind of guys Coach Saban loves to recruit. Ha Ha and Vinnie always got excited for me during practice whenever I had success—if, say, I got my footwork right or applied some of the things they were teaching me. That's how you can tell if someone is a true leader: they get excited about others' successes. They got excited about mine, and it meant the world to me.

As the season rolled around, however, it felt as if I was back in the same place I had been a year before. We had a highly touted recruiting class in addition to the returning starters who had been a part of our national championship team, and it was once again extremely difficult to dress for games and break into the lineup.

Midway through the season, I had dressed for a couple home games, but it looked like my chances of playing would be slim. Because of the widespread talent on our team, it was beginning to feel like an impossible climb. This forced me to ask myself some difficult questions.

To be candid, I started having doubts about playing for the University of Alabama. It had nothing to do with the coaches or the players or the program—I loved it there—but I was becoming restless over my lack of playing time. I had known coming in that it would be difficult to break into the lineup as a walk-on, but not playing for my second year in a row was still a tough adjustment. Dressing for some of the games was cool and all, but when you've been a starter since you were twelve, well, it's hard not to be out there on the field. I was antsy. Ready to play. Ready to help the team not only in practice but also during games. It was frustrating to feel like I was progressing so much in practice but then fail to see any fruit for my efforts on the field. Of course, my expectations might not have been realistic for a walk-on, but it was what I felt nonetheless.

One weekend when the team was on the road, I remember returning to Centreville for the weekend and having a serious conversation with my parents about potentially transferring to a smaller school for my junior season where I could get immediate playing time. Mom and Dad listened to me and comforted me in my discouragement.

When I returned to Tuscaloosa on Sunday evening for our five o'clock team meeting and workout, I saw a piece of paper resting on my passenger-side floor as I pulled up to the football complex. Parking my truck in the players' lot, I picked up the piece of paper and read it. It was a handwritten note from my father.

Taylor,

Just remember: God is on your side. If God is for us, who can be against us? (Romans 8:31).

- *God will open doors for you. Be patient. Trust Him.*

- *Pray for this. Pray for your coaches!*
- *Pray for your teammates.*
- *God has a plan for you! (Romans 8:37–39)*

Love you!

Dad

Considering the discouraged state I was in, the note was perfectly timed. Dad's words reminded me that I was playing for more than just myself. I was playing for God and for my team and for my family. I was playing for Trent. Quitting—well, not really quitting but leaving Alabama—would go against the one thing my brother left me. How hypocritical would it have been for me to walk away from Alabama just because it was challenging?

The principle most deeply ingrained in the culture of Alabama football was the idea that we were not playing for ourselves, yet this was the principle I most struggled to integrate. Dad's note reminded me not only of the message I preached but also what playing for Alabama was all about: selflessness. We were playing for each other. For our fans. For the community. For those who needed hope, an escape. It wasn't about me. It was never about me.

Instead of exhausting myself focusing on the fruit of my labor or lack thereof, I decided I would shift my thinking and focus on the beautiful, sanctifying process of the journey. How was I growing? What was I learning? Who was I becoming?

As I walked into the facility, I had a rejuvenated spirit within me. This was where I was going to play college football for the rest of my career—here in Tuscaloosa—whether I got onto the field or not.

Once I went all-in with playing for the University of Alabama, it seemed that my relationships were taken to another level. This seems natural since I was thinking less about myself and more about the overall good of the program.

My relationship with Coach Cochran, for example, continued to develop in meaningful ways. That's not to say he took it any easier on me in practice—if anything, he was harder on me because it gave him more of an acute eye for how I was playing—but off the field, it wasn't uncommon for us to have conversations about faith or family or how things were going with my speaking engagements. He always seemed especially intrigued with the things I was working on outside of football, like Converge and my speaking.

When I had left Centreville the year before, I wondered if I'd be able to keep doing the things I was doing—like working with Converge and scheduling speaking appearances—because I knew that playing for Alabama would be a full-time job. It was tough to juggle all these things, especially without getting paid to speak, but Coach Cochran's support of me was just another reminder that the coaching staff at Alabama primarily cared about who and what their players were becoming. Both of these ambitions of mine were positive things, and the coaches supported me as I pursued them.

Daddy Jim had said when I signed with the University of Alabama that I'd have a larger platform for Jesus being a walk-on at Alabama than being a star player at any other school, and I was finding his prediction to be accurate. Local media outlets were beginning to hear about my story, and Tuscaloosa businesses and schools were beginning to contact me, interested in having me speak to their employees and children, respectively. The buzz in Tuscaloosa eventually led us to move our annual Converge conference to T-Town. All of these things were encouraging to me because my deepest desire was for people to know about Trent and be inspired by the life he lived—and perhaps experience the love of God in hearing about Trent and how my family responded to the tragedy.

Some of my teammates began to confide in me, as well. Earlier that October, one of my teammates and friends, Daniel Logan, a walk-on freshman from Coppell, Texas, received a call from home notifying him that his little brother had died. His brother, Jacob, only one year younger than Daniel, was a senior at Coppell High School and a standout wide receiver for their football team. He was reportedly cliff jumping with his friends at Possum Kingdom Lake in Texas when he drowned. Divers found his body four days later.

Daniel went back to Texas and ended up missing a month or so of the football season, but we exchanged a number of texts and met up when he returned to Tuscaloosa. I think he chose to confide in me because he knew I had lost my brother as well.

"Don't let anyone tell you it's okay because it's not," I said. "How you respond to this will determine your outlook on the rest of your life."

I never tried to explain to Daniel why God would allow something like that to happen nor did I tell him that things were going to be okay. There were so many similarities between Jacob's death and Trent's death—them both being one year younger than us and both dying in such unexpected manners. It's a pain no loved one should have to experience. I wanted Daniel to know that I was there for him.

On the field, the 2012 season mirrored the season before. We won our first nine games, which included victories over No. 8 Michigan, No. 13 Mississippi State, and No. 5 LSU. But at the beginning of November, we once again lost at home, this time to quarterback Johnny Manziel and No. 13 Texas A&M.

Following our loss to A&M, Coach Saban wasn't as fiery as you might expect. In the locker room following the game, he simply told us, "Get ready for practice on Monday. We're moving on to the next opponent. Learn from this and put it behind you. Don't dwell on it."

I think Coach knew that the campaign we had put together, like the year before, was strong enough to result in another national championship berth—that is, if we could finish strong.

We won our next three games, including a 32–28 victory over No. 3 Georgia in the SEC Championship Game at the Georgia Dome. And, as some might have predicted, we were once again given an opportunity to play for a national championship. This time, it was against Notre Dame at Sun Life Stadium in Miami.

I think we were ultimately given another shot because of our stellar finish to the season and because of our 3–0 record against Top 10 opponents. The entire year, we once again showcased a dominating defense, one that gave up an average of only 10.7 points per game.

For the BCS National Championship, Alabama once again took two planes so everyone on the team could dress. It was just as neat as the year before and brought back some of the same feelings. Could we really win two national championships in a row?

Upon arriving in Miami, we checked into the Fontainebleau, a beachfront hotel in South Beach, one of the nicest hotels in the country. Walking in felt like being in a James Bond film or something, which is funny because the hotel was featured in *Goldfinger* in 1964. When I got to my room, I could see the Atlantic Ocean from my window.

Celebrities were everywhere at the Fontainebleau. Days before, the rapper Drake had performed on the poolside stage outside the Fontainebleau for a New Year's Eve pool party. One day, we met ESPN basketball announcer Dick Vitale. Another day, we met singer Sean Kingston, who said something along the lines of, "You Bama boys know how to do it." Hearing something from a celebrity like that was weird because it was like, for a minute, we were on his level. I got a picture with him, too.

A number of stories came out that week raising questions as to whether or not the Fontainebleau would be a distraction, and an ESPN college football analyst blasted our program for staying there. What people don't realize, however, is that we were assigned to the hotel, and our entire team was together in a separate wing. It's not like we were scattered throughout the whole building. Some of the ballrooms on that wing were turned into meeting rooms and locker rooms, and the hotel was transformed into a football facility of sorts. Anyone who thought that Coach Saban was losing control of his team and allowing us to lose focus obviously didn't know Coach Saban.

That entire week, we only went to the beach once, and we had a strict curfew of eleven o'clock each evening. By "strict curfew," I mean that Alabama personnel checked our rooms each night at eleven, and if a player didn't make curfew, then he was asked to pack his bags and was sent back to Tuscaloosa on a Greyhound bus. No exceptions. Again, it was a business trip, just like Coach Saban always preached.

The game was held on Monday evening at Sun Life Stadium, the home of the Miami Dolphins, and it featured a record-breaking Sun Life crowd of 80,120 people. It seemed like there were actually more Notre Dame fans than Alabama fans. Although the game the year before had been labeled "The Game of the Century," this year's national championship was also historic because it featured two of the most storied football programs in the country: the Fighting Irish, with eleven claimed national titles, and us, with our fourteen claimed titles.

We entered the game tied with Notre Dame with eight *Associated Press* titles. Facing the Irish this time around would be an opportunity to avenge Bear Bryant's 24–23 loss in the 1973 Sugar Bowl to Ara Parseghian's Fighting Irish team, which resulted in the *Associated Press* ranking the Irish No. 1 in the country. My role would be minimal, but it was incredible to be a part of such a historic game. The rivalry probably meant even more for my dad, who grew up watching those legendary Alabama and Notre Dame teams.

Speaking of Dad, he was once again at the game—along with my Mom, T.J., and a couple friends. They all sat in the Crimson Tide family section in the north end zone. To once again have them there in attendance meant the world to me.

Any skeptics who thought we might have lost focus staying at the Fontainebleau were soon to find out how silly their assumption was. Like the year before, we came strong out of the gates. We scored on our first three possessions of the half and our last possession of the half, as Eddie Lacy ran all over the Irish and A.J. McCarron completed any pass he wanted. Overall, we shut out Notre Dame and entered halftime with a commanding 28–0 lead.

We ran into the locker room at halftime to the sound of our fans chanting, "SEC! SEC! SEC!"—implying that no other conference in the country was even comparable in strength. To be honest, it already felt like we had won the game. In the locker room, we were all pretty amped up, and it felt like an extremely loose environment.

That's when we witnessed Coach Saban storm into the locker room and start yelling at us, the maddest and most fiery I had ever seen him.

"This game is NOT over!" he yelled.

Apparently, he didn't like the loose vibe in the locker room.

I'll say it again: Coach Saban is a mastermind at keeping his team focused.

He set us all straight real quick, explaining that whenever you have momentum and are moving fast, you can't take your foot off the gas until the race is won. Coach sensed that we were slowing down and coasting, and he wouldn't tolerate that mindset.

The result of Coach keeping us mentally dialed in was a 42–14 victory, our second national championship in a row. Eddie Lacy was named the game's offensive MVP, and C.J. Mosley was named the game's defensive MVP.

As great as the celebration was the year before, I enjoyed it even more my sophomore year. I was more relaxed with who I was on the team and more comfortable in my role. Once again, I felt such a great sense of accomplishment—that the reason we worked so hard throughout the year was for a moment like this. Here we were again. We did it.

I ran around the field for a while with my teammates as we received black 2013 BCS National Championship snapback hats and were handed newspapers featuring the front page of *The Birmingham News*, which read "BAMA AGAIN!"

Roll Tide.

Next, in a moment of elation and praise, I ran to the north end zone and climbed over the wall to find my family in the stands. The fans loved it as players, one by one, filed over the wall to be with them in the stands.

Once I made it over the wall, with the help of stadium security lifting me up from below and fans pulling me from above (I'm short), I navigated my way through the stands and found my family. They were all smiling, and I hugged each one of them. It was a beautiful moment.

Dad was the last person I embraced.

He pulled me in and said, "Great job, son."

23
Breakthrough

"If you hold that football long enough, it will become a part of you."
~Bear Bryant, Alabama head football coach (1957–1983)

"You see the giant and the shepherd in the Valley of Elah and your eye is drawn to the man with sword and shield and the glittering armor. But so much of what is beautiful and valuable in the world comes from the shepherd, who has more strength and purpose than we ever imagine."
~Malcolm Gladwell, best-selling author

The year before in New Orleans, I stayed out all night with my teammates. In Miami, however, I went back to the Fontainebleau after the game and went to bed.

As strange as it might sound, I think that Coach Saban's mindset was beginning to become ingrained in me. You work hard to achieve something. You achieve that something. You enjoy that something you've achieved, for a moment or so, and then you start focusing on achieving something else. Going to bed that night, I was obviously elated, and I felt very blessed to be a part of the University of Alabama at such a unique time, but I was also looking ahead to the future.

When we landed at the Tuscaloosa Regional Airport the following afternoon, we were greeted by hundreds of Alabama fans. A week later, there was a parade on University Boulevard. Two months later, we once again went to the White House, this time presenting President Obama with a white #15 jersey. (Interestingly, we were all at the White House on the day of the bombing at the Boston Marathon, which put a damper on the celebration.) A couple weeks later, there was the grand reopening of our football facility after its nine million dollar renovation. And then, just like that, it was once again time for A-Day and the receiving of our national championship rings.

Heading into A-Day, I felt like a veteran. I had two seasons under my belt and was about to enter my third. The playbook, by this point, had become second nature. Like Bear Bryant had told my father in elementary school, Alabama football had become a part of me.

In our 2013 A-Day, I played more of a role on the field than I did the year before, which I found to be encouraging. I also got to bite my teeth into a juicy steak after a solid victory for the White Team over the Crimson Team. Best of all, we were given our rings after dinner.

Throughout the remainder of the spring, I met one-on-one once or twice a day with our new defensive backs coach, Greg Brown, who Alabama had hired in January when Jeremy Pruitt accepted a position on Florida State's coaching staff. Meeting one-on-one with a coach so frequently was something I wasn't accustomed to, and it led me to believe that he had big plans for me on the special teams unit that fall. He really seemed to invest a lot in me.

This, combined with having a more active role in our A-Day game, made me think that my shot was coming. I just knew it.

As ready as I felt, it also seemed that the coaches were ready, too—ready to give the walk-on a shot on the field.

Something funny and interesting—and I guess "weird"—happened after spring training in May. . . .

As usual, we were given a break at the end of May to recuperate before summer workouts began in June. I had conveniently scheduled all my speaking engagements during this break, so I returned to Centreville with plans of traveling to a different high school or church just about every day. Since winning a second national championship, my story had picked up even more speed in the central Alabama area. On a side note, it's interesting how our culture works—how "two-time BCS National Champion" next to my name somehow suddenly gave me more credibility, even though my story was pretty much exactly the same. But I wasn't complaining. I just wanted people to be encouraged and strengthened by my story and by Trent's legacy.

During this time, I often found myself thanking God for bringing me to Alabama and for expanding my platform of influence, even though my role was minimal in our two national championships. At the same time, I knew I had come a long way since thinking about transferring a year before. Whenever I visited a church or a school, it was neat to see the look on kids' faces as they held my national championship rings. Working so hard, day after day, was worth it just to see those kids' faces glow.

One of my speaking engagements was at a church in Pinson Valley, just north of Birmingham. My little brother T.J. came with me, and on the hour-drive to the church, I felt a sharp, unexplainable, and unbearable pain in my stomach.

"Man," I told him, "I'm going to need you to drive. I'm hurting."

T.J. was only fifteen at the time with a learner's permit, so he was scared to drive on the Interstate. I actually don't even know if he was legally allowed to drive with anyone other than Mom or Dad. But I was desperate.

"Are you serious?" he asked.

I think he was caught off guard. He wasn't used to hearing me complain, and he certainly wasn't used to seeing me in pain. Weakness was an uncomfortable thing for me to show to anyone, especially a family member.

"Yeah, man," I said, pulling the vehicle over on the side of the road. "I need you to take me to the emergency room."

T.J. maintained his composure and drove me to the nearest emergency room. I don't even know where it was.

While I was there, doctors gave me some medicine and took an X-ray of my stomach. Nothing showed up on the X-ray, which I supposed was good, and the doctors told me that it was probably a severe stomach virus. This was encouraging because as bad as I was hurting, I feared that it might be serious.

"Well, what do you say we still go to Pinson so I can speak?" I asked T.J.

"Are you serious?" he said again.

"Yeah," I said, "let's go."

We eventually arrived at Pinson Valley, and when it came time to speak, I took a trashcan onto the stage with me and told the crowd that I had the stomach flu and that there was a decent chance that I might puke during my talk. And I did. About twenty minutes into my story, I couldn't hold it, and I walked over to the corner of the stage and threw up. In front of everybody. Luckily for those in attendance, I wasn't wearing a mic because that would have sounded horrible blasting through the speakers. After I puked, I felt fine. Those in attendance had to have been thinking to themselves, *This guy is insane.*

I found it ironic that in two years with the Crimson Tide, enduring some of the most brutal workouts in the blistering heat under Coach Cochran, I didn't puke once. And yet, here I was, puking for the first time in who knows how long—in front of a live audience.

"You're crazy," T.J. told me after my talk.

Then we drove home to Centreville, where I also spoke at the Bibb County Relay for Life that evening in the old gymnasium at the high school.

Just another day in the office.

In June, summer workouts began once again, and I officially entered my junior year. It's crazy to think that the only thing I had experienced in my first two years at Alabama was winning national championships. I knew nothing else. My fellow juniors and I entered the year ready to win another one.

I mentioned that I felt like a veteran at A-Day, and it was a similar feeling during the summer workouts. I think that one of the reasons that I felt so confident as we transitioned into another season was that I was in the best shape of my life. For two straight years, I had conditioned under Coach Cochran and lifted under Coach Cochran, and I had access to some of the best nutritionists, trainers, and methods in the country. On top of that, I hadn't undergone any serious injuries in two years with the Crimson Tide, so I'd been able to progress without taking any steps back.

What people might not realize is that all of this combined really adds up over time. I had entered Alabama weighing 190 pounds, and now I weighed 215 pounds. Because of the caring, brilliant professionals and coaches involved in the Alabama football program, I had added twenty-five pounds of pure muscle. I was benching approximately 405 pounds.

Through high school, I had always worked out and considered myself to be "in shape," but Alabama and its methods had a way of taking physical fitness and nutrition about fifty steps further. Day by day, they gradually turned their players into physical freaks. My point is that I felt experienced and more ready than I had ever been—ready for a breakthrough year and hopefully a third national championship.

24
Those Three Words

"If you have a beautiful story, it has to have conflict. If you don't have conflict, it can't be a good story."
~Donald Miller, author and speaker

I woke up in the middle of the night on June 19, 2013, with a horrible feeling in my stomach. There was nothing unusual about the day, but there was something very unusual about the feeling.

It had been just another typical day for a UA football player: football, class, and football. That morning, I went on a run with the team; that afternoon, I attended my Human Development class; that evening, I went back to the football facility for seven-on-seven drills. After practice, I went out with some of my teammates to one of UA's dining halls, and not long after dinner, my stomach started to hurt. It was painful, but it wasn't unbearable. I figured it was once again the stomach flu, just like a few weeks before, because the feeling was similar.

I called my girlfriend, Linlee, who was over an hour away in her hometown of Clanton. She and I met in high school and dated off and on throughout college. She recommended that I drink a Sprite and eat some crackers. I did. And I felt a little better. Why Sprite and crackers were supposed to make me feel better, I had no idea.

When I woke up in the middle of the night, however, I was experiencing an entirely different level of pain. It felt like a knife was being jabbed into my back. Not to sound dramatic, but part of me did think that I might be dying.

I'm not going to the hospital, I said to myself. I had workouts the next morning and just wanted to get some rest.

I lay in bed for a while, tossing and turning and thinking about how maybe I should've drank more Sprite or eaten a few more crackers. That would have helped.

The pain, however, became unbearable. Even more unbearable than the time T.J. drove me to urgent care before my speaking engagement at Pinson Valley.

I had to swallow my pride and find a way to the hospital.

My roommates were asleep, and I didn't want to bug them. They would be annoyed. There was no sense in calling my girlfriend because, as I mentioned, she lived over an hour away. There was no point calling any of my teammates because they had to wake up early the next morning for workouts, and I didn't want to appear weak in front of them. And I definitely didn't want to call 911—that seemed too dramatic.

So, in a panic, I called my friend Megan. She had been one of my best friends in college since my freshman year; she lived nearby, and I knew she would pick up her phone.

"Hello?" she said wearily.

"Megan," I said. "Look, I need you to come get me and take me to the hospital."

"Are you serious?" she said.

"Yes," I said, "I feel like I'm dying."

"You *better* be dying," she said. (Megan liked her sleep.)

In minutes, Megan was outside my apartment complex. I had chills like never before, so I threw on two hoodies, even though it was the middle of summer, and I made my way down the two flights of stairs in my apartment complex to the parking lot, holding my stomach.

When Megan saw my condition, she quickly exited her car and tried to help me.

"I'm fine, I'm fine," I said, denying her help.

And I got into her car.

By the time we arrived at DCH Emergency Room, it was around two o'clock in the morning. I felt like I was a pregnant woman being rushed to the hospital, with something within me about to burst.

The doctors fed me some pain medications and made me drink some nasty-tasting dye before my CT scan. If you could take a bundle of chalk, put it in a blender, and turn it into liquid, well, that's how the dye tasted. Awful. They suspected I might have appendicitis, so the dye would help them more clearly see the pictures taken during the scan.

When they shot the dye into my body, my whole body went warm, and I felt like I had peed myself. I didn't, thank goodness.

At five or six o'clock in the morning, doctors confirmed that I had appendicitis.

"We're going to perform surgery in two hours," the doctor told me.

The first question I asked him was, "So I guess I won't be making workouts today, huh?"

The doctor laughed.

After talking to the doctor, I was encouraged that the appendectomy was a standard procedure and that my recovery wouldn't keep me from football for too long. It was only a minor surgery; therefore, it was only a minor setback.

I wondered if this was why my stomach had been hurting so badly a few weeks before on the way to Pinson Valley. Urgent Care doctors had told me it was just the flu; now, it seemed that those doctors were wrong.

The first person I called after being informed that I had appendicitis was Coach Cochran. I didn't want him to wonder why I wasn't at practice that day. When I told him the news, his response was, "Yea-yea-yea-yeaaaaaaaa!" as if he was pushing me during a sprint workout or something. "You'll be fine!" he said, motivationally. "We'll catch you up! Get better!"

His inspirational tone reinforced everything I had been feeling. I was ready to put this behind me and get onto the field. This was going to be my year.

After talking to Coach Cochran, I figured I should probably call my mother since she had no idea I had been at the hospital all night.

Needless to say, she was not happy when I informed her that I had been at DCH for hours and was about to head into surgery. She definitely thought I was joking when I first told her.

Once I convinced her that I was telling the truth, she and my family and a few friends from church hightailed it to Tuscaloosa to be there with me before the surgery, which I appreciated. Several of the athletic trainers came over to the hospital, too. The procedure was only an appendectomy—it wasn't a huge deal—but it was still nice to feel the overwhelming support of friends, family, and the Alabama football program.

The appendectomy surgery was successful.

I was in a bit of pain after the procedure, but compared to the pain I was experiencing before and the pain I experienced each day at practice, any soreness I felt after the surgery is hardly worth mentioning.

I did, however, give the nurses a scare immediately following the operation. Still somewhat weary from the pain medications, I fell asleep in my hospital room, and before I knew it, the nurses were waking me up in a panic. I had no idea what was going on or why they woke me up in such a startling fashion, but I would later find out that they thought I was dying when they heard the *beep-beep* of my electrocardiogram slow to dramatic levels, like forty beats per minute (the average is sixty to one hundred beats per minute).

They thought my heart was shutting down.

They would find out that this was due to a combination of two things: one, being in such a deep sleep, and, two, being in such good cardiovascular shape from playing on Alabama's football team.

When I was released from the hospital later that day, I had one thing on my mind: getting back to doing just that—playing football.

I knew that I faced at least two weeks of recovery. As the first few days passed, the competitive spirit within me hated not having the opportunity to get better while everyone else was progressing. But that's just part of being injured. It happens. And most players deal with it at some point in their careers. Now it was my turn.

We were given a few days off during the week of July 4, so I met my family down at Gulf Shores to hang out with them. Linlee came along, too. It had been a week since my surgery, and I was already feeling a lot better. I was even playing volleyball at the beach. I was aching to get back onto the football field, and in some ways, I felt like I already could.

Unfortunately, I had to cut my beach trip and family time a little short because I had a follow-up appointment in Tuscaloosa with the surgeon who had performed my appendectomy. As far as I knew, I was progressing fine, but I hoped to receive some encouraging news regarding my progress.

The day of my appointment, Linlee and I left Gulf Shores in the morning and made the four-and-a-half-hour drive back to Tuscaloosa for my check-up at the Northport Medical Center. When it came time for me to meet with the doctor, Linlee remained in the waiting room as I was escorted to a standard patient room. I was casually sitting on top of one of those thin paper linings on a hard hospital bed when my doctor walked into the room. The first thing he said was, "Are your parents here?'

A little caught off guard by such a strange question, I laughed and responded, "I'm twenty years old. I usually just come to the doctor's office by myself."

I wasn't trying to have an attitude, though it might have sounded that way; I just thought it was an odd thing for him to ask.

"Well," he responded, "this is serious."

"Okay," I said hesitantly, caught off guard again. "What's going on?"

"The appendectomy went great," he told me, sitting down. "We got your appendix out before it burst. You're good. The issue is that we found a tumor attached to your appendix and your colon. The tumor inside of you isn't benign—it's malignant."

I stared blankly at him, trying to comprehend everything he was telling me.

"You have cancer," he said.

25
Built by Bama

"The ultimate measure of a man is not where he stands in moments of comfort and convenience, but where he stands at a time of challenge and controversy."
~Martin Luther King, Jr., civil rights hero

Those were the last words I expected to hear. When I went to the doctor that day, I was hoping to receive some good news about my progress and an update about playing football, but in an instant, playing football became the furthest thing from my mind, which was odd because football had consumed my life for the last two years.

It's difficult to explain what runs through your mind when you hear those three words, "You have cancer." In some ways, it was similar to receiving the shocking news six years before that Trent had died in a tragic accident. There was no time to prepare, no time to grieve in that moment, nothing you can do—it just becomes your reality. And you adjust. It's the only thing you *can* do: adjust.

I had known people who had cancer, mostly older people, but, just like losing a sibling, you never expect it to happen to you. When it does happen to you, it's almost impossible to comprehend—that this is your reality now, your cross to bear, your fight to fight.

When my doctor gave me the news, I had no idea what kind of questions to ask or what type of cancer it was or how serious it was. All I heard was the word "cancer," and the only thing I wanted to do was be with someone.

"Do you mind if I bring my girlfriend in here?" I asked.

"That's fine," he said.

I exited the patient room and walked down the unfamiliar hospital hallway, probably in a flustered daze, past the nurses and doctors and patients and into the waiting room.

"Hey," I told Linlee. "Can you come in here with me?"

"Why? What's up?" she asked.

"My doctor just told me that I have cancer," I said, stone-faced, showing little emotion.

"Stop," she said, as if she thought I was joking.

"No, I'm serious," I responded. "Come with me, for real."

She quickly got up from her seat and followed me back to the patient room, where the doctor explained everything to her—that during my appendectomy the surgeons had found a cancerous tumor attached to my colon.

I had cancer inside me. At twenty years old.

Linlee and I just kind of looked at one another as if to say, "What now?"

"We need to call your parents," the doctor advised.

I was hesitant. I didn't want to call my parents, who had just lost their son six years before, to tell them that their oldest son had cancer.

But the doctor was right, of course; I needed to tell my family. I just knew they had already been through so much, and I didn't want to tell them.

Eventually, with the help of the doctor, we called Mom. The doctor talked first. Though he did a great job of thoroughly explaining everything to her, she was understandably shocked. The doctor eventually handed me the phone, and Mom said to me, "We're packing up and leaving the beach right now. We'll see you soon."

"Okay, everything is going to be fine," I assured her, downplaying it all. "This isn't a big deal."

After talking to my girlfriend for a while in the hospital room, my doctor returned to inform me of some things and to give me some direction.

"I'm going to set you up an appointment with an oncologist," he told me.

"An oncologist?" I questioned. "I'm not a girl." (I was thinking of a gynecologist.)

"This is a cancer doctor," my doctor laughed.

And so it was settled: in three days, I would see an oncologist.

I wasn't in the best state of mind upon leaving the hospital, so my girlfriend drove us back to campus. I don't remember much about our conversation on the way back to UA—I was still in a state of shock. But I remember her telling me, "I don't want to lose you."

"Well," I said, "we don't know what's going on yet. We'll get more details after my appointment."

She wasn't crying or anything. It didn't seem like everything we had just experienced at the hospital was real. Did I really have cancer? Was this some sort of nightmare? Would I be waking up any second?

"Where do you want me to drop you off?" she eventually asked me, as we approached campus.

"I need to go to the football facility," I said. "I need to see the coaches and trainers."

I needed to be with my Alabama family.

My girlfriend dropped me off, and I entered the newly remodeled facility and went directly to the athletic training room. The facility was quiet and empty, as the majority of the players were still on their July 4 vacation. The environment was void of its normal hustle and bustle, which felt kind of eerie.

Entering the training room, I saw Jeff Allen and Ginger Gilmore. I'm sure they could tell something was wrong with me because I struggled to say what I wanted to say and ended up choking over a bunch of words that I'm sure made no sense at all.

It was beginning to hit me. Something about being back in the facility—surrounded by all the history and tradition, all the glamour, all the pride, all the accolades detailed in art throughout the building—made me realize how all of it could be taken away in an instant. I had invested my life into football, and now it seemed like I could lose it all.

Struggling to speak, I gave them a piece of paper that I had in my pocket that stated that I had an appointment with an oncologist.

Jeff and Ginger seemed shocked as they read over the piece of paper, and they asked me a few questions about my diagnosis that I tried to answer. It was a broken moment, but the compassion they had for me in my situation was encouraging to me.

Eventually, Jeff asked if they could pray for me. I thanked him and told him I would appreciate that. So there, in the University of Alabama training room, standing on the center of the Alabama "A" stitched in the carpet, Jeff and Ginger placed their hands on me. Jeff prayed, "Father, be with Taylor. We pray for Your healing and that you will give the doctors and nurses wisdom. Please strengthen Taylor, and we ask that You comfort him and give him peace in this difficult time. Amen."

They were there for me—not just as a football player, but as a person they deeply cared about, a person they loved. Whatever lay ahead of me, I knew I had the full force of my Alabama football family behind me.

As we said our "amens," I felt strengthened. I knew I wasn't alone. I would defeat cancer and return. I would kick its butt and pick back up where I left off. I would complete the climb I so desperately wanted to make as a walk-on player on a team of superstars.

I gave both Jeff and Ginger a hug and told them I was going to find Coach Cochran.

Coach Cochran's door was open, as always. I knocked, and he welcomed me in. "How'd the follow-up appointment for the appendectomy go?" he asked, as I sat down.

By this point, my mind felt clearer.

"Well, everything was good," I said, "but they found a tumor and they say it's cancerous. I am going to see an oncologist in a few days to see what the next step is."

Whereas Jeff and Ginger were somewhat shocked, Coach Cochran, as I might have expected, entered all-out attack mode.

"Man, you're *strong*," he said. "You got this. If this was going to happen to anyone on the team, anyone in this organization, you're one of the few people who can get through it. You can handle it."

I nodded, and I again felt comforted by Coach's words. I think our personalities always meshed well because we had similar responses to pain. *Press through. Take it on. Attack.*

"Hey, you're in the best shape of your life," he continued. "Whatever you have to do—surgery, chemo, whatever it is—you can handle it.

You're going to be fine. Get ready to take this head on."

"That's what I'm gonna do, take it head on," I said.

"That's right," he said. "Let's go. Man, you got this."

After talking a while more, I thanked him for his counsel, gave him a hug, and told him goodbye.

"We're going to take care of you here," he concluded.

"All right," I said. "I appreciate ya, Coach."

26
Attack Mode

"When something happens to you, you have two choices in how to deal with it. You can either get bitter, or get better. I chose to get better. It's made all the difference."
~Donald Miller, author and speaker

"Don't give up. Don't ever give up."
~Jimmy Valvano, author/speaker and North Carolina State basketball coach who lost his life to cancer

When I left the Alabama football facility, I was ready to take on cancer right then and there. I felt strengthened by my Alabama football family; it was as if my visit to the facility breathed life back into me. I was ready. Determined. This was just another opportunity to express what I truly believed and to never quit in the face of adversity. Everything I preached, everything I stood for, was coming full circle. Whatever happened, whatever lay before me, I was ready to, as Coach Cochran said, "take it head on."

It was hard to believe, when I left the facility, that it wasn't even yet mid-afternoon. What a long day it had been already. From driving back to Tuscaloosa from Gulf Shores that morning to being blindsided with the news that I had cancer to visiting the Alabama football facility and having my spirit rejuvenated . . . all I could say to myself was, "What a crazy day." I felt more optimistic and had accepted the journey that lay ahead of me, but I was exhausted.

I went back to my apartment, and my childhood friend Anna Michael came over with her new golden retriever that was only a puppy. She had learned the news when my parents had told the Oakleys. Playing with the dog, simple as it may have been, seemed to help me get my mind off things for a little. When Anna Michael came over, I was reminded of the time she came over to my family's house in Centreville six years before, when Trent had passed away.

My family returned to Centreville the following day, and I joined them at home.

Of everyone, I would say that my family took my diagnosis the hardest. Considering what they had already been through, this wasn't a surprise. Though I was obviously bummed about the fact that I had cancer, I was sometimes more downtrodden for their sake—I hated seeing them go through something that was so dramatic and serious again. After what they had already been through and suffered and will forever be suffering through, I felt like they should never have to deal with any type of trauma again.

Of course, life doesn't work like that. But I do believe they will have a special place in heaven for all they've endured and how they've placed their trust in God's promises in the midst of it all. Once more, because of the example they set for T.J. and me when Trent passed away, I found myself drawing strength from their faith in the new battle I faced.

Expectedly, they had all sorts of questions for me about my diagnosis. I couldn't answer most of them. We ended up researching all kinds of stuff about cancerous tumors on the Internet, which was a little nerve-racking at first, but we found out that if I was going to have cancer at my age, then this was the best cancer to have, as strange as that might sound.

We still didn't know if I'd have to have surgery or enter chemotherapy, but the cancer I had, according to the Internet, was not as dangerous or fatal as most. This gave me a sense of hope and peace. To get our minds off of things, we actually went back down to the beach that same day. My cousin Jeremy came with us, and it was nice to escape a bit and relax my mind.

I'm not going to act like I didn't have some dark moments and thoughts as my cancer became more and more real to me. Like anyone, I had times when I naturally got down about my situation. I prayed some prayers, asking God why I couldn't have a normal life like everyone else and why nothing seemed to come easy to me. In my darkest moments, I thought about the people I knew who had died from cancer like my grandfather.

Whenever I found my mind adopting a victimized or fear-based mentality, however, I tried to redirect my thoughts. I tried to, as 2 Corinthians 10:5 says, "take captive every thought." The truth was that I was a blessed child of God, because He had lavished His grace upon me. He had provided me with a life to live and an eternal home that I did not deserve. Though life had its challenges, I had already been blessed with every spiritual blessing in the heavenly realms because I was united with Christ (Ephesians 1:3). Plus, quite practically, it's more common to live a life filled with pain than one without any pain. As long as this fallen, sin-stricken world is spinning, we will face adversity time and time again.

The negativity I battled in my mind the most involved football. The timing of my diagnosis couldn't have been worse. Before my appendectomy, I remember excitedly telling my parents how I thought I was finally going to get a chance to play on the field during my junior campaign. I told them how the coaches were investing in me .

"I think they have big plans for me," I told them.

Now, though I hated to admit it, I knew that my cancer diagnosis was a major setback to getting on the field my junior year. It wasn't out of the question, and I was indeed optimistic, but I knew it'd take a storybook comeback.

Again, however, I knew I couldn't stress out about something like that. Everything was what it was. I could get bitter or better. I could think about the frustrations of not playing, or I could start making my comeback, which began with meeting with my oncologist on Monday.

It was weird walking into the Lewis and Faye Manderson Cancer Center at DCH Hospital on Monday morning. I was too old to go to the children's cancer wing, so there were elderly people all around me in the waiting room. I do not mean for this to sound insensitive, but it felt like these people were nearing the end. Some of them, sadly, were in really poor shape. It was sobering and eye-opening. As I sat there, comforted by the presence of my family and friends, I kept looking around. It was odd to be surrounded by so much frailty and weakness. It was strange to have gone from Alabama football conditioning—with some of the most talented, strongest college football players in the country—to this.

I couldn't help but think to myself: *I'm not supposed to be here.* And it was as if the older people in the room knew it, too; I was definitely getting some curious looks as I sat there. There was nothing hereditary about my cancer, nothing age-related, and nothing that had to do with my overall health because I felt great. It all seemed so bizarre.

All of this only enforced what I'd been feeling since my diagnosis: *Let's get this over with and get the heck out of here.* I was prepared to accept whatever news my doctor gave me. Whatever I needed to do, I was ready to do it.

After going over all my information, my cancer doctor told me that she was going to have the surgeon who had performed my appendectomy perform another surgery on me in the coming days: a right hemicolectomy, which would basically be the removal of the right side of my colon in an attempt to make sure the cancer didn't spread to my lymph nodes. If it had already infected and spread to my lymph nodes, it would then inevitably spread throughout the rest of my body.

"If this was a benign tumor, we wouldn't even do the surgery," she said. "But since it's malignant, we have to perform the surgery because of the fear of the cancer spreading."

If the surgery was successful, I would technically be cancer-free and would therefore not have to undergo chemotherapy or radiation.

"This is all very strange and different because you are so young," she said. "So we have to take all the precautions."

Though they said it was a pretty dangerous procedure since they would be rerouting my colon, I still considered everything my oncologist told me to be great news. I didn't have to do chemo—not yet, at least. And there was a chance that the surgery could take care of everything. I hate to say that I was excited, but I really was: I was excited to get it over with and move on with my life.

The surgery was scheduled for a week and a half later, and I began counting down the days.

27

'Every Bama Man's Behind You'

"Yea, Alabama! Drown 'em Tide!
Every Bama man's behind you,
Hit your stride."
~Alabama Fight Song

The night before my surgery, I stayed at home in Centreville. I had to bathe with a specific lotion, which would somehow help prevent me from getting an infection when the doctors made an incision in my stomach.

I woke up the next morning at four thirty to make the drive from Centreville to Tuscaloosa. I do not know why, but I insisted that I drive even though my parents offered to drive me. Looking back, I think I was desperate for some sense of control. I felt blindsided by the entire ordeal—going from being on the brink of breaking into the Alabama lineup to all of a sudden having to have surgery to remove the cancer that I never knew I had. I didn't want to feel helpless, like I couldn't take care of myself or something. So, as silly and stubborn as it might sound, I drove to Tuscaloosa that morning on my own. And it felt good to do so. My family followed behind me.

All of us arrived at the hospital at around six o'clock. As the eight o'clock surgery approached, a few more people came to my private hospital room. Two pastors from Centreville Baptist, Ken Fuller and Chuck Oliver, visited my room and prayed with me before the surgery, and Sharon Oakley dropped by, too. I had undergone minor surgeries before, but I knew this one was a bit different because I would be in the hospital for a few days. I really appreciated everyone's loving support. There was definitely a different vibe to a surgery as serious as this one. Lots of papers had to be signed. More precautions. More medication.

Finally, at around eight o'clock, the nurses began rolling my bed toward the anesthesia room. While they were doing this, though I was pretty drugged up, I remember seeing one of my old buddies from Centreville, Lee, who I hadn't seen in years. I was so confused because he was the last person in the world I expected to see.

"Lee?" I questioned.

"Whoa! What's up, man?" he said.

I would later find out that he was in the hospital because he sold medical equipment for a living or something like that. Whatever the case, it was super random, and I thought I was dreaming.

Before I knew it, one of the anesthesiologists was peering over me, saying, "Count to ten."

"One," I counted, "two, three," and then everything faded to black.

It felt like I had woken up in hell.

I was apparently in a recovery room of sorts because there were patients in beds all around me, separated by curtains. All I heard were chaotic screams and anguished cries—over and over, seemingly never-ending—because of the pain they were experiencing.

My mind was in a fog, so I fell back asleep, only to wake up to the same disturbing noises a bit later. I fell asleep once more, only to wake up to the exact same thing again.

By this point, I was wide awake. There was no going back to sleep. I wanted to. But I couldn't. The surgery, as I would find out, lasted three and a half hours, so by this point the anesthesia was wearing off rather quickly. My mind spinning, I tried to patiently wait for the cries and screams to stop, but they wouldn't. They only seemed to grow louder, as if someone was slowly turning up the volume dial, and I began to notice the specific details of people's cries—the long, low moan of the man to my left and the piercing screech of the woman to my right. The man to my left said something like, "I think I'm dying," while the woman to my right sounded as if she was being tortured, like the pain medication was not working or something. It was truly horrifying. I have witnessed a lot of people's reactions to pain, but I've never heard anything else like that.

Most would probably consider me to be a pretty laid-back guy, but I found myself becoming restless and anxious. The cries wouldn't stop.

I felt like I was going insane. This probably only went on for ten minutes or so, but it felt like I was in that room for an eternity. I would later find out that I was in the recovery room for an hour and a half because they were trying to find me a private room where I could stay for multiple days.

A nurse eventually walked by, and I got her attention.

"You *have* to get me out of here," I said, "even if you have to put me out in the hallway for a little."

"Okay," she said. "We'll try to get you a room."

A nurse eventually wheeled me out into the hallway and into the relieving silence. As she moved me, I realized how much pain I was experiencing. It felt as if there were a thousand needles inside me pushing into my stomach. It was nice, however, to leave that horrible recovery room.

"Thank you," I mumbled to the nurse.

"You're welcome," she said. "You have some people here to see you."

She pushed me past the waiting room, and that's when I saw a sea of people—coaches, players, trainers, friends, and family—all standing up and cheering for me as I went by. I felt so moved and inspired, like I had just walked through the tunnel at Bryant-Denny on game day.

As much pain as I was in from the surgery, I'm not sure I felt any of it in that moment. If I hadn't been so drugged up, I might have been emotional enough to actually cry for once. As the nurse pushed me away, I made a number one sign with my finger.

28
Twenty-Five Pounds

"Scars are tattoos with better stories."
~Anonymous

"Without your wound, where would your power be?"
~Brennan Manning, author of *The Ragamuffin Gospel*

The nurse wheeled me to a private room, my home for the next four or five days.

The doctors explained to my family and me that the surgery had been successful. They had removed the malignant tumor and rerouted my colon. Now, it was a waiting game. They had sent part of my colon off to a pathology lab to see if I was cancer-free. Pathologists had to run tests to see if the cancer had spread to my lymph nodes. The scariest thing about the cancer spreading and hitting the lymph nodes is that it can quickly and aggressively spread to the heart and lungs.

They also explained that there was a two-and-a-half-inch deep cut in my stomach and that I would have to get a series of shots every morning and every evening to help prevent clotting. Those shots became my least favorite parts of the day. As brutal as Coach Cochran's two-a-day conditioning sessions might have been, I would take those, even in 110-degree weather, over two-a-day shots any day. As you can imagine, the feeling of a thousand needles pushing against your stomach is only amplified when there are actual needles going into your stomach.

Before leaving my room, the doctor mentioned that the results from the pathology test would be back by the end of the week. Until then, I would have to recover and wait.

I had been in my new room for twenty minutes or so when one of the nurses asked me, "Do you want me to ask everyone in the waiting room to leave?"

I think she could tell I was in a lot of pain.

"Heck no," I said. "Bring them in."

I didn't know if I'd be much company, but I was overwhelmed by everyone's love and support—that all those people in the waiting room came to check on me—and I definitely wanted to honor their time. I didn't want them to feel bad for me at all, but I wanted to express to them how thankful I was that they were supporting me.

The nurse hesitantly acknowledged my plea and then slowly started welcoming people into the room. She could probably tell right away that I was going to be a handful and would probably push the limits in an effort to undergo a quicker recovery. And she was right. The surgery was over, and I was ready to conquer the next step, whatever that was—whether it was chemo, radiation, or working my way back onto the football field. I was ready for anything. I just wanted to make progress.

Friends and family began to trickle into my hospital room. It was a humbling experience to see them come in one after another, and I was once more reminded of the value and meaning that is experienced in relationship with others. Six years before, the town of Centreville had rushed to my family's aid upon hearing the news about Trent, and now many of these same people, along with my Alabama football family, were rushing to my bedside in the midst of my physical trials.

Later that same day, my nurse asked me if I needed a catheter to help me urinate.

"Heck no!" I told her.

By this point, I think the nurse was beginning to understand how stubborn of a person I am; I didn't want the help of anyone or anything. Plus, there was no way I was going to use a catheter before the age of eighty. Not a chance in the world.

However, I hadn't urinated since my surgery, so the nurse told me that I had two hours to urinate in a plastic jug by my bed or the catheter would be the only option. Is there anything more horrifying than the thought of a catheter?

After she said that to me, something as simple as urinating became one of my primary concerns and goals for the day. Two or three weeks before, the main goal in my life was to break into the University of Alabama's starting lineup; now, it was to pee on my own terms. Life has a funny way of making you appreciate the simple things. And no, I never had to use a catheter—thank goodness.

I learned a lot that day. Though I did not like feeling weak and broken, both feelings were important reminders that I was in desperate need of both God and people to truly be strong. My tendency as a man and as a Division I football player was to do everything I could to be strong on my own—or at least to project to others that I was strong on my own—but after a major surgery to remove my cancer, I was left with hardly any physical strength.

In short, all this was a vivid reminder that I couldn't be strong on my own because I am naturally weak, broken. In this case, I was broken because I had cancer. But on a much deeper level, I am broken because I am a sinful man who needs grace. And I desperately need God and His people to help strengthen me.

I was reminded of 2 Corinthians 12:9: "But he said to me, 'My grace is sufficient for you, for my power is made perfect in weakness.' Therefore I will boast all the more gladly about my weaknesses, so that Christ's power may rest on me."

Something else that came to my mind while I was in the hospital that day was the process that muscles undergo when they are put through a difficult workout. First, the myofilament fibers in a muscle are *broken* down; however, that does not mean the muscle is weak—rather, it means the muscle is becoming stronger. This is how I tried to approach the broken state I was in: *I was becoming stronger.* Could it be that this whole ordeal was a demonstration of God's grace, because He was molding me into the person He wanted me to be, making me stronger, sanctifying me, and refining me?

All in all, that first day in the hospital was a humbling experience. There were people hanging around in my hospital room until midnight. A lot of people texted me, called me, or posted something on social media about my surgery. Even West Blocton High School, our rivals at Bibb, posted a picture on social media of a sign in their weight room that read, "Standing Tall for Taylor." My phone was blowing up all day.

Along with family and friends, several of my teammates also dropped by after my surgery. Coach Cochran had apparently told the entire team that morning, "Be praying and thinking about Taylor today; he has a big surgery."

Knowing how demanding and consuming the schedule is for Alabama football players, it meant the world to me that my teammates reached out to me the way they did.

Before some of my teammates left the hospital that day, they told me that they couldn't wait for me to be out there on the field with them again.

And I assured them I'd be joining them soon.

The following day was much like the first. It seemed like every ten or fifteen minutes someone new walked into my room.

My parents were obviously around the most, and I think it was comforting for them to see all the support I received from the Alabama football program. I think one of their fears for me as a walk-on was that I might be forgotten or left behind as I lay in a hospital, unable to contribute to the team. I hadn't been to practice in two weeks, and I had to drop out of one of my summer classes. Going from two-a-day practices, summer school, and practically living at the football facility to this—two surgeries in two weeks and living in a hospital—made me feel extremely removed from the University of Alabama.

But I wasn't forgotten in the slightest bit. At other programs, this might have been the case. Far too often in athletics, a player is unfortunately only worth the value of his performance. And as far as performance goes, an injured walk-on has to be near the bottom of the totem pole. But at Alabama, so many teammates and coaches dropped by to show their support or called me to check up on me. Coach Cochran once told my mother during this time, "He's going to be taken care of. Don't worry about him. We take care of our own."

This was demonstrated from the very top—from the trainers, the coaching staff, and all the way up to Coach Saban. In practice, Coach

Saban was a motivator and a perfectionist; in my situation, he was a comforter and an encourager. He was extremely concerned and had all kinds of questions for me about my surgery, how I felt, and the next step in my recovery. I told him I didn't know if the cancer had been removed but would find out in the coming days.

The goal the day before had been urinating without the help of a catheter, and on the second day, the nurse challenged me to sit up in my hospital bed and try to move myself down to a chair.

That's a dumb goal, I thought to myself. *To sit in a chair?*

I decided to see if I could do more. So instead of sliding down into a chair, I forced myself to walk to the door and back, holding onto my IV pole and rolling it beside me as a crutch. The nurse looked at me as if to say, "You can't just take it easy, can you?"

I guess my point in telling this silly story is that I was restless and helpless—restless to get moving, get out of the hospital, and get a move on with my life again, and helpless because I couldn't. Life was on pause. So were my dreams and aspirations. I struggled to be still, and I hated being idle. My surgery and my recovery forced me to do both.

This feeling only worsened over the next few days. I might have gradually become more mobile, but I was still extremely limited in where I could go and what I could do. I knew in the back of my mind that the quicker I could get out of the hospital and conquer cancer, the quicker I could get back to playing football. But the whole process felt painstakingly slow. And it had only been a week!

In my past, my response to pain always involved doing something about it. Talk to someone. Help someone. Take something bad and use it for the good of someone else. Sitting in a hospital bed, unable to do anything and reliant on people to take care of me, was torturous for me.

However, like most unfamiliar feelings or uncomfortable situations, I learned a lot about myself. In fact, it is through unfamiliarity and discomfort that God can do some of His best work. Author and speaker John Maxwell says, "If we're growing, we're always going to be out of our comfort zone." Here I was, with no other option but to be patient in my idleness and stillness. It was such a difficult thing to swallow my pride and realize there was nothing I could do in my own power to get better, but it was also such a freeing thing to realize that I was entirely dependent on the One who held my present and my future in His hands.

Like anyone else, I felt most at ease when I had control of my life, but realizing I wasn't in control, as scary as it was, seemed to be even more freeing because, in my smallness, I could see His magnitude; in my weakness, I could see His strength; and in my questioning, I could cling to His truth.

My brokenness led to God's promises, and believing in God's promises led to hope. Without brokenness, it is difficult for us to awaken to the treasure of hope.

One of the verses that comforted me during this time was Proverbs 16:9: "In their hearts humans plan their course, but the Lord establishes their steps." I had plans of having a breakout year on the football field, but God had determined my steps. It is much better to have God guiding your steps, though the path might be tumultuous, than to determine your steps on your own, which is a quick path to destruction.

I was thankful for the promises that God revealed to me—these promises that would mold me into the man He wanted me to become, even if it hurt. Without a wound, there is no healing; without a scar, there is no story; and without trials and conflict, we cannot possibly relate to others and encourage them.

Maybe becoming like Christ in my pain, enjoying Him in my pain, and glorifying Him in my pain, was more important than anything else on this earth I could possibly attain—even more important than my football ambitions.

As my week in the hospital came to an end, my family and I anxiously awaited the results of the pathology test. I was curious to see whether I would enter the fight against cancer or whether I could focus on fighting my way back onto the football field.

Whatever the future was, I knew the fight was going to be difficult. Cancer would be difficult, obviously, because it's cancer. Working my way back into football would be difficult because of what my body endured, not only during the procedure but more so in my recovery.

Between my hemicolectomy and my week-long recovery in the hospital, I had lost *twenty-five* pounds. In a single week, I had gone from 215 pounds, in top-notch physical condition, to 190 pounds, which was what I weighed as a senior at Bibb County. While I was in the hospital, all I could eat was chocolate pudding and ice chips—for five days straight. Going from two-a-day workouts, a top-notch weight-lifting program, and the careful care of Alabama nutritionists and trainers, to being completely idle, weak, and only able to digest chocolate pudding was a hard fall that I hadn't anticipated.

But I also knew that my trial would only make my story greater because of the conflict in the story. It would only strengthen my testimony because of the tests I had endured. And grace would ultimately shine brightly because of the brokenness I had experienced.

The Friday I was scheduled to be released, Mom and Dad were in the hospital room with me, and my doctor came into my room sporting a gigantic smile. That's when he delivered the news my family and I had been longing to hear: "The surgery was successful, and the tests came back negative. Taylor, you are cancer-free."

29
The Long Road Back

"Life is a gift, and it offers us the privilege, opportunity, and responsibility to give something back by becoming more."
~Tony Robbins, motivational speaker

What I went through isn't comparable to what most of the cancer patients I know have been through. My cancer might have required a serious surgery, but I never had to go through chemotherapy or radiation. It might have altered my plans, but I was never legitimately afraid for my life. My heart goes out to anyone who has had to face cancer or anyone who lost a loved one to cancer. As the late ESPN host Stuart Scott, who died of cancer in January 2015, once said, "When you die, it does not mean that you lose to cancer; you beat cancer by how you live, why you live, and in the manner in which you live."

The glimpse of cancer I was given, however, forever changed me and continues to change me today. In many ways, it was another reminder of the frailty and brevity of life. Much like Trent's tragedy, it was a reminder of how quickly something can be taken away and how quickly your life can change. James 4:14 says that our lives are "like a mist that appears for a little while and then vanishes." This is why it's imperative to make the most of each moment, to seize each opportunity, and to notice and respect each person you meet.

Most importantly, my experience gave me a heart for those afflicted with cancer. When I think of people who truly live out the phrase, "Never, never quit," I think of those who are fighting cancer, young or old, male or female. Those people inspire me more than any celebrity, athlete, author, or pastor.

In the summer of 2014, I spoke at a back-to-school bash at a church in Amory, Mississippi. That's where I met a girl named Serra Pearson, a fifteen-year-old girl who had been diagnosed with a rare form of cancer called AAG (autoimmune autonomic ganglionopathy).

First off, I wasn't even supposed to speak in Amory that day. Two weeks before, I had met a motivational speaker from the Air Force named Lacy Gunnoe at a book-signing event for author and pastor Acton Bowen, a mutual friend. Lacy and I had a good conversation that day at the bookstore, and I could immediately tell that he would become a close friend. A week later or so, Lacy was unexpectedly deployed, and he asked me if I could fill in for him at his speaking engagement in Amory. I told him I could.

And that's where I met Serra.

When I arrived at the church, I saw a girl hooked up to an oxygen tank and sitting in a wheelchair. I approached her and introduced myself.

"I'm Serra," she said.

She smiled and shook my hand.

After the event ended, we talked longer, and I learned that doctors estimated that she only had two weeks left to live; they hoped she would live through her sixteenth birthday in September, three weeks away. This was very saddening to me, but as we talked, I began to realize that Serra was one of the most joyful, bubbly girls I had ever met—despite her tragic circumstance. She had an unspeakable joy about her that transcended life and pain. She opened up to me about her disease and, having heard my talk that evening to all the students in attendance, she said to me, "I don't know if God is going to heal me on earth or in heaven, but if it's in heaven, I will tell your brother that you said 'hello.'"

I found her to be truly inspiring. Before I left, I gave her a "Never, Never Quit" wristband and T-shirt, and we agreed to stay in touch.

Over the coming weeks, Serra and I talked or texted every single day. I encouraged her, she encouraged me, and we became very close. Day in and day out, she fought for her life. One day, she went into the hospital for her usual tests, and the doctor was surprised that her lungs were yet to shut down. (Most with her condition wouldn't be able to breathe by this point in the journey because the disease would have deteriorated their lungs.)

"I don't know what's going on," the doctor said, stunned.

"I do," she said. "I have a God who is bigger than anything I can imagine."

Before we knew it, her birthday had arrived. My girlfriend and I drove out to Amory to surprise Serra at her party, and there were probably over five hundred people at her house. It was a gigantic celebration, most likely her final birthday.

Serra kept fighting. She fought AAG through October, and one day it dawned on me to capture her story on video in order to inspire others, just as she had inspired me. She loved the idea and agreed. So one weekday morning at the beginning of November, her family brought her to Tuscaloosa, and we filmed her talking about her journey and sharing her faith. For lunch, I took her to Taco Casa, a staple in Tuscaloosa, and that evening, I escorted her to the Alabama football facility, where she was able to watch a practice and meet some of the coaches and players.

Two weeks later, she passed away.

I was asked to speak at her funeral, and I remember driving from Tuscaloosa to Amory trying to figure out what to say. When she died, a part of me died as well. It was the most difficult time I'd had to speak since Trent's funeral seven years before.

I think that having had cancer myself helps me better relate to people like Serra and helps them relate to me. As much as I enjoy meeting and journeying through life with people like Serra, it takes a piece of me away when they die. Life is too short for some people. Serra was only sixteen years old.

To this day, Serra Pearson and her story continue to inspire people through the video we filmed and the life she lived.

If I could somehow talk to her today, maybe she would tell me that Trent says "hello" back.

Upon being told I was cancer-free and being released from the hospital, I knew in the back of my mind that it was still unlikely that I'd play football my junior season. But I could hope. And I could work hard.

When I had entered the hospital, I knew I was about to undergo a major operation, but I never fathomed I would lose that much weight in such a short time frame. Maybe this was ignorant, but losing twenty-five pounds in a week was beyond my comprehension.

I had only faced one injury since my freshman year of high school, and that was a broken wrist. The thing about my wrist injury was that I could still run, lift, and even play on game day. Now, however, I couldn't do anything. I was weak. The weakest I'd ever been.

On top of that, when I asked my doctor about my future in football, he told me that even once I gained my strength back, he would still be ultra-concerned about me getting hit in the stomach. It would take a long time for everything inside me to fully heal. But I wasn't ready to give up on football. I would cross that bridge and weigh the risk of getting hit once I worked my way back into the physical form I'd been in before the surgery. One step at a time.

All we get is one life to live, and in my life, I wanted to play football, even if it was risky. So my primary goal became working my way back, and I hoped I could progress enough that maybe, just maybe, I'd still be able to play my junior year.

I began taking any step I could to live normally again. The day after I was released from the hospital, five days after my surgery, I was scheduled to speak at a nearby church. I didn't want to cancel on the church nor did I want to feel helpless. So I had Jeremy drive me there (I couldn't drive because of the pain medication I was taking), and I spoke on stage with a pillow wrapped around my stomach. It was pretty painful, and I was forced to talk more softly, using my Presbyterian voice instead of my Pentecostal voice. I was gassed when I was finished. If anyone was in attendance who had also happened to see me puke on stage a few weeks before, they must have thought I was a total mess.

After spending the weekend in Centreville under the care of my family, I decided that I wanted to go back to Tuscaloosa on Monday. I was limited, and I probably could have used a couple more days of rest, but I wanted to get a move on with my life.

The first thing I did upon arriving in Tuscaloosa was visit the UA football facility. A number of people said something to me like, "We're not used to seeing you like this," or "This isn't the Taylor Morton we know." I still had a pillow strapped to my stomach, and I obviously couldn't run or even lift the bar in a standard bench press, which was quite a blow since I had been benching 405 pounds before my surgery. That summer, I had even beat Coach Cochran in the "dip game," where you go head-to-head with someone else to do as many triceps dips as you possibly can. "You can probably beat me now," I joked with Coach

Cochran.

Still, as bizarre as it felt to suddenly be unable to do a single physical thing, it felt good to be back home.

My first day back, I made my usual rounds. I talked to Jeff, Ginger, and Coach Cochran, and, as always, I felt very encouraged by what they had to say—I was optimistic about the future.

Next I headed upstairs and asked Coach Saban's receptionist, Miss Ashley, if Coach was around. Miss Ashley told me he was in his office.

Upon seeing me, Coach—dressed in his traditional khakis and salmon-colored Alabama golf polo—immediately walked over with a big grin on his face and welcomed me into his office. If you've never seen Coach's office, I highly recommend looking it up on the Internet. It's immaculate. It has the appearance of a log cabin or a cigar room— pinewood style floors; a tiled, dark walnut ceiling; wooden bookcases, shelves, and display cases lining both sides of the room; mahogany furniture; and a massive cherry desk with an Alabama Crimson Tide logo carved on its front.

Attached to his desk are his three Alabama national championship rings encased in a glass display box, and he even has a button that opens or closes his door from his desk. On the back wall is a massive window with crimson curtains, and in front of the window sits a wooden hat rack—his iconic, straw, practice hat resting on top. In short, his office looks the way you would expect his office to look, considering he's one of the best coaches in college football.

Coach guided me to a conference room attached to his office, where we sat down at a huge, sixteen-person wooden table. We talked for thirty minutes or so, and none of it had to do with football. He just wanted to make sure I was okay.

It is moments like these where Coach Saban's love and support for all his players is truly evident. And when I say "all his players," I mean *all* his players. Not just the starting quarterback. Not just the guy who is going to get drafted into the NFL. His love and support extended even to a walk-on like me.

I left his office encouraged, strengthened and even more inspired and motivated to bounce back and perhaps help Coach Saban add a fourth Alabama ring to his collection.

A couple weeks later, I was finally able to get rid of that irksome pillow. Soon after, I began walking on a zero gravity treadmill, which allowed me to improve my endurance a bit without putting any additional pressure or strain on my stomach. Four weeks later, right around the start of the season, I got my stitches removed and was told that I no longer had to drain my insides, which had been a daily routine. (Yes, it was as disgusting as it sounds.) I was finally also able to start lightly jogging on the zero gravity treadmill, and my doctors said I was progressing nicely.

It was around this time, however, when reality began to sink in. Though my recovery was going as well as it could go, the doctors said I had another six weeks before I could lift, and they also warned me that I needed to ease into running.

As difficult as it was, I began to accept that my junior season was a wash. I might have had the mindset and the goal to return for our 2013 campaign, but there was no way I would be able to handle a usual team workout, let alone compete once again for a roster spot. I guess my initial timeline for recovery had been a bit ambitious.

Soon thereafter, I met with Coach Cochran, and we discussed the inevitable—that I wouldn't be able to play my junior season.

"Ya know," Coach Cochran said, "I've been thinking a lot about your role on the team this year, just in case you couldn't play. I was wondering if you'd like to have sort of a 'player coach' role this year? It'll be more responsibility, but I think it could be a great opportunity for you to learn about coaching."

Without hesitation, I jumped at the opportunity.

"Of course," I told him, "I'd love that."

And so it was settled: for the 2013 Alabama football season, I would be a player coach for the Crimson Tide.

Being a player coach was entirely different than any other football experience I had at Alabama—or in my entire football career, for that matter.

I never realized how intricately detailed coaching can be, even in something as simple as running a drill in practice. I had to be in the right place at the right time, attentive to the direction of Coach Saban or the assistant coaches, in order to relay the proper messages to the players I was directing. If I couldn't follow the instructions as a coach? Well, that just wouldn't look good. Being a coach, there was even more pressure for perfection and more of a need for accountability.

Every challenge, however, is an opportunity to grow. And I definitely grew that year, more than ever before. Coaching required more responsibility and, all in all, required more time. I was asked to run drills in practice, attend some meetings, and assist the coaches in various tasks.

This is why it's difficult to explain what exactly my responsibilities were: I was doing just about everything. Being in a coach's role, I realized that everything the coaches did was for the betterment and progression of the players. It was nothing personal. It was all to make the player better, and, most importantly, to benefit the Crimson Tide.

I enjoyed learning, especially from Coach Cochran. Almost every day, I would talk to him about a variety of things. We were already close, but we got *really* close during the 2013 season. We spent so much time together.

What I enjoyed most about the opportunity was the aspect of servant leadership. Every day, I read the same quote from student leader Brent Crowe that I had plastered on my apartment mirror: "Leadership starts at the feet of Jesus." My role, each and every day, was simple: serve the coaches and serve my teammates, whatever that meant.

When you're a player, everything kind of revolves around you—your wants, your needs, your progression, and your development. But as a coach, you realize that it's not about you at all—it's about doing everything you possibly can to make your players better and to give them a positive, though challenging, experience playing for Alabama.

Overall, I loved being around the game and being involved in football once again. Football is the best game there is, and it teaches so many life lessons. Never have I had a coach that *didn't* impact my life in some way. Now, I hoped I could impact the players that the coaches entrusted me to guide. I really enjoyed coaching, and I knew that if I ever wanted to pursue the profession, Coach Cochran would help me any way he could.

Throughout most of the season, it looked like we might become the first team in the history of college football to win back-to-back-to-back national championships. We were ranked No. 1 in the country the entire season, carding stellar victories over No. 6 Texas A&M, No. 21 Ole Miss, and No. 10 LSU. In the final game of the season, however, in the Iron Bowl against our rival, No. 4 Auburn, on the road, we were on the unfortunate end of one of the most shocking, stunning plays in the history of college football. I do not even feel like explaining what happened. We all know what happened by this point. If you haven't seen it, you can look it up yourself. And if you are an Auburn fan reading this, I certainly do not want to give you the pleasure of reading an Alabama player's description of a 109-yard touchdown run off a missed field goal attempt with no time on the clock to win the game.

Auburn went on to defeat Missouri in the SEC Championship and then went on to lose to Florida State in the BCS National Championship. Deflated from our loss to Auburn, we went to the Sugar Bowl in New Orleans, where we lost to No. 11 Oklahoma.

Unfortunately, after winning consecutive national championships, the only way to back that up was by winning another one, which had never been done before in the history of the BCS era. At some point, you kind of become entrapped by your own successes because there is no room for improvement, only a standard to be upheld. It was a frustrating finish to the season, falling to both Auburn and Oklahoma, but all you can do is press forward.

While helping the coaches throughout the season, I also continued to progress as a player. By mid-season, I was running once more and no longer using the zero-gravity treadmill. And a little after that, I was finally cleared by doctors to lift. It took a long time for me to be cleared because of all the internal healing that had to take place. Still, it felt good to start making progress again.

Toward the end of the 2013 regular season, I remember one of my teammates, Dillon Lee, asking me, "When are you coming back?"

"I hope next year," I told him.

Getting back into conditioning and lifting was a freeing thing because I felt like I could start building toward something once more, but it was also a frustrating thing because of the strength I had lost. I was nowhere near the physical condition I had been in before my surgery; having my stomach cut open had knocked me back twenty steps.

I was amazed at how far I had fallen.

But determined to work my way back up.

30
One for a Thousand

"Don't ever discount the wonder of your tears. They can be healing waters and a stream of joy. Sometimes they are the best words the heart can speak."
~Paul Young, author of *The Shack*

As I explain all this, I understand that it might sound as if my football career was too far gone to regain. I get it. Not only was I still weak, but there was also the existing risk of getting hit in the stomach. This was a looming reality that I tried my best to ignore.

Moving past the Sugar Bowl and stepping into January 2014, however, the concern of getting hit was brought to the forefront as I began thinking about my senior season. If I continued to move forward as planned, my first physical contact on the gridiron since my surgery was right around the corner, most likely in the spring. Was it worth it?

I knew all along, as I awakened more and more to how weak and limited I really was (and how serious my surgery had been), that it probably wasn't the smartest thing for me to keep playing. But I couldn't bring myself to walk away from the game. I couldn't bring myself to give up my dream. I simply loved playing football way too much.

Ever since Trent had passed away seven years before, football had been my escape from a world of pain. It was an avenue of expression, a chance to communicate the things that I struggled to explain. Football allowed me to experience so many positive things: meaning, purpose, camaraderie, victory, and the general feeling that I was accomplishing something. All of this was essential for me in high school as I tried to cope with the death of my brother. Football was also a mission field for me—a platform for me to share my story and a chance to influence people and share true hope and genuine joy with them.

Moving into college at the University of Alabama, football became a lifestyle, which I had no problems with because I loved the game enough to make it my lifestyle. Being part of something that was so much bigger than myself—a program with one of the best traditions in college football, that preached selflessness and sacrifice, that I had pulled for since as long as I can remember, that my father had pulled for ever since his youth when he was granted an opportunity to meet Coach Bear Bryant—had been the best experience of my life, and I wasn't ready to give it up.

There, playing for Alabama, I had met lifelong friends and learned some of the most valuable lessons I could ever learn. The program, the lifestyle, my coaches, and my teammates were all factors that made it difficult to let go.

When I returned in January for the second semester of my junior year, one of the first things I wanted to do was talk to Coach Cochran about my future. We were about to transition into a new season, and I wanted his opinion. How did he think I was progressing? How much further did he think that I had to go? Where did I have to improve to get back into the mix of things?

My first day back on campus, I went to the football facility and started talking to Coach Cochran by the nutrition bar, where he had told me three years before that I needed to pick it up or that I wouldn't last very long. I expressed to him my goals, now that my year working as a player coach was over, and we began discussing my future on the Crimson Tide.

"Ya know, Taylor," he said, "honestly, you have a bright future in speaking. You have a lot of awesome things going on right now in your life. And the risk of you coming back and playing football is bigger than the reward can be. You would have to start from scratch, and doctors are worried you are going to get hit."

He seemed to imply that I needed to start thinking about my future career, not just playing for the Crimson Tide.

I nodded. I couldn't say I disagreed with him. Coach Cochran was right. He basically verbalized all the doubts I had, all the doubts I was running from. I knew working my way back was an uphill and risky climb.

Coach Cochran explained that I could keep coaching, too, but he also warned me of the lifestyle and its demands. After a year of being a player coach, as much as I enjoyed it, I knew coaching was not something I wanted to pursue in my career, at least for a little while. I had more of a passion for speaking and for Converge.

Still, the decision was mine. Should I keep coaching? Should I try to play? Should I walk away?

"It's really up to you," he continued. "You choose. I will support you no matter what you decide, but I think you will be better off getting away from football this year."

Coach Saban always talked about how he was preparing us—his players—for the day when someone would tell us, "You can't play football anymore." This was the underlying principle behind Coach Saban's philosophy for the program: to build boys into men and release them into the world to have a positive impact on society. And it was as if Coach Cochran was doing just that—releasing me into the world—even if it meant losing the only thing that I wanted: football.

The rest of the day, I took some time to think about Coach Cochran's words and pray about my future. Slowly, I began to believe that Coach Cochran was right. Maybe my football career at the University of Alabama was over.

Sure, it didn't have to be. I could keep coaching or try to play. I had entered my meeting with Coach Cochran dead set on playing football my senior season. But Coach Cochran, a man who I trusted with my life, had given me the advice and counsel that, though I might not have wanted to hear, was something I *needed* to hear.

There was nothing for him or the program to gain by recommending that I hang up the cleats; I was only a walk-on, and they weren't paying me to coach. Plus, Coach Cochran said he would support me no matter what I decided. The decision was in my court. I knew that Coach Cochran's words came from the bottom of his heart, and I was beyond confident that he had my best intentions in mind. Considering how much I trusted Coach Cochran, his advice was impossible to ignore.

Even though walking away from the game would be the hardest

thing to do, I became convinced that it was the right thing to do. It was as if I just knew Coach Cochran was right. The thought of making a return to football had consumed my mind ever since I found out that I needed an appendectomy seven months before; but now, my future seemed to become crystal clear in an instant, even though I had no idea what it would entail. It was an odd, sobering, freeing thing to have such a revelation, and it was something I never would have seen if Coach Cochran hadn't spelled it out for me. It's difficult to explain, but somewhere deep within me, it felt like a chapter was closing.

It was time to walk away from football. It was over.

Later in the day, I drove home and retired to my room in silence. And, for the first time since the World Changers conference in Tampa, Florida, seven years before, I cried.

I had never felt such a conviction.

Around this time, my friend Lacy Gunnoe, who I mentioned earlier, told me, "This isn't a career-ending injury; it's a career-starting injury." That's what I was trying so desperately to believe, that though one door was closing, maybe a thousand doors were opening—in ways that I could not understand.

Two or three days later, I went to the facility and had my name removed from the roster. I cleaned out my locker and gathered my belongings, including my jersey and my helmet.

Before I left the facility, Coach Saban said to me, "Come by whenever, Taylor. You'll always have a place here."

31
Those Three Words

"Never, never quit."
~Trent McDaniel Morton

The fall of my senior year at Alabama, I returned to Centreville one Friday afternoon. The Choctaws were playing West Blocton, our rival, on the road that evening, and my little brother, T.J., was a junior on the team. I was excited to watch him and my former school play the game I missed.

It was different attending football games now—no longer having a connection to the sport, no longer playing. I felt so removed from the game. Sometimes I wondered if playing for Alabama had been a dream. So far that fall, it had been difficult to watch the Crimson Tide play; in some ways, I still felt like I should be out there. I was yet to watch a game from the stands at Bryant-Denny, and I hadn't watched a single game on television. I knew that walking away from football had been the right decision. Health-wise, it just wasn't worth the risk. But I missed the game with all my heart. To be honest, it still hurt to let it go.

I had already returned home for a couple Bibb County games that fall (I had a lot more time on my hands), and watching the Choctaws play always seemed to send me into a reflective state. It had been four years since I had worn the purple and gold. And since graduating from Bibb County, I had been a part of two national championship teams at Alabama, gotten cancer, defeated cancer, and walked away from football. What a whirlwind.

I loved coming home to watch the Choctaws play, but for some reason, I never liked watching the games with people, as weird as that might sound. Not even my family or friends. I don't know why. I just wanted to be alone and think and watch the game with no distractions. So I usually watched the games from the fence behind the end zone.

That night against West Blocton was no different. I stood there all evening, leaning against the fence, listening to the Choctaw band in the stands behind me, taking in the game, watching my brother play, and letting my mind wander through the ups and downs of the last eight years.

And then I began to think about Trent.

Maybe he was why I liked being alone at the Bibb County games—because it was here, on the football field on Friday nights, where I felt closest to him. Maybe I wanted to experience that mysterious closeness once more—through a sport that had been my escape from pain for so many years but also something that helped me cope with loss and move through grief. God used football to help me heal. For this I was thankful.

What would Trent be like if he were here today? It's a hard question to answer, but it's a pleasant thought to have. Because this is how I feel close to him now. Through reliving past memories. Through sharing my story. Through getting lost in my imagination.

I'd imagine Trent would be a junior in college, probably majoring in something related to science. Maybe he would have joined me at the University of Alabama and roomed with me, like we were kids again. If that were the case, I'm sure we would have spent plenty of afternoons throwing a baseball back and forth on the Quad, and I'm sure we would have spent plenty of evenings playing video games into the thick of the night, procrastinating our homework.

Or maybe he would have attended the school he adored the most, LSU, just as I had attended Alabama. Maybe he would have even received a basketball or baseball scholarship to represent the Tigers. Maybe our friendly sibling SEC rivalry would have been heightened. Maybe he'd be standing next to me on the fence line, decked out in LSU gear. That wouldn't surprise me at all.

No matter where he might have gone to school, I know he would have been sitting in the stands at both national championship games. And I know he would have been as captivated as he was when Dad took him to a Tiger game for the first time, the year before he died. And I know those victories would have meant even more than they already did—because my whole family would have been there.

But April 1, 2007, changed all of that. And that's okay. Because life has a way of doing that—of changing. And it's okay to not be okay with it, and it's okay to place our faith and hope and trust in God anyway. This is what I have chosen to do, because faith must involve the unseen world to be faith at all.

Whatever the case, I miss him. But I'm thankful he's happy now, as happy as he'll ever be. In heaven with Jesus.

Late in the fourth quarter, the Choctaws trailed their rival by a point, with one last opportunity for the offense to complete a game-winning drive. You could almost feel the mixture of anxiety, excitement, and restlessness in the crowd—the confusing hum of mixed emotions. And that's when I heard something unified beginning to build in the Choctaw band behind me.

The Choctaw fans joined in, and I smiled as a familiar chant once more rose into the autumn, Alabama sky.

"Never, never quit."

SOURCE MATERIAL

Chapter 1

"Given the choice between the experience of pain . . ." from *The Wild Palms* by William Faulkner, Vintage Books, 1995, copyright 1939 by William Faulkner.

Chapter 2

"Christians never say goodbye . . ." from *The Captive Bride (House of Winslow Book #2)* by Gilbert Morris, Bethany House, 2004.

Chapter 3

"This is the end—but for me . . ." from *Bonhoeffer: Pastor, Martyr, Prophet, Spy* by Eric Metaxas, Thomas Nelson Inc., 2011, page 528.

Chapter 4

"The death of a beloved . . ." from *A Grief Observed* by C.S. Lewis, Zondervan, 1989.

"The work of restoration cannot begin . . ." from *The Wounded Heart* by Dan Allender, NavPress, 1990.

"I thought I could describe a state . . ." from *A Grief Observed* by C.S. Lewis, Zondervan, 1989.

Chapter 5

"Death is not the end but is really a transition . . ." from "Could You

Pray Three or Four Times an Hour?", *BeliefNet*, and available at http://www.beliefnet.com/Faiths/Christianity/2005/01/Could-You-Pray-Three-Or-Four-Times-An-Hour.aspx?p=3

"You cannot always control what happens . . ." from *Be A People Person: Effective Leadership Through Effective Relationships* by John C. Maxwell, David C. Cook, 2013, page 26.

Chapter 6

"That life only really begins when it ends here on earth . . ." from *Bonhoeffer: Pastor, Martyr, Prophet, Spy* by Eric Metaxas, Thomas Nelson Inc., 2011, page 531.

Chapter 7

"In some ways suffering ceases to be suffering . . ." from *Man's Search For Meaning* by Viktor Frankl, Beacon Press, 2006.

"Pain has a way of clipping our wings . . ." from *The Shack* by William P. Young, Windblown Media, 2008.

Chapter 8

"All is grace . . ." from *All Is Grace: A Ragamuffin Memoir* by Brennan Manning, David C Cook, 2011, page 27.

Chapter 10

"My home is in heaven . . ." from *Hope for the Troubled Heart: Finding God in the Midst of Pain* by Billy Graham, Harper Collins, 2011.

"There is an endless kingdom to be enjoyed . . ." from *Pilgrim's Progress* by John Bunyan, Harper Collins UK, 2013.

"You're born. You suffer . . ." from "Billy Graham's Home Field Advantage," *Christianity Today*, June 20, 2005, and available at http://www.christianitytoday.com/le/2005/june-online-only/cln50620.html

Chapter 11

"Regardless of what you want to do or who you are . . ." from *Start* by Jon Acuff, Ramsey Press, 2013.

Chapter 12

"The death of the Beloved bears fruit in many lives . . ." from *Life of the Beloved: Spiritual Living in a Secular World* by Henri J.M. Nouwen, The Crossroad Publishing Company, 2002.

Chapter 13

"The decisions you regret in life . . ." from *Unplugged* by John C. Maxwell, The John Maxwell Co., 2011.

Chapter 14

"While other worldviews lead us to sit . . ." from *Walking with God through Pain and Suffering* by Timothy Keller, Penguin, 2013.

"I am certain that I never did grow in grace . . ." from *Spurgeon's Sermons on Great Prayers of the Bible* by Charles H. Spurgeon, Kregel Academic, page 31.

"Grace doesn't depend on suffering . . ." from *The Shack* by William P. Young, Windblown Media, 2008.

Chapter 15

"It's okay to not be okay . . ." from *All Is Grace: A Ragamuffin Memoir* by Brennan Manning, David C Cook, 2011, page 107.

"In Alabama, there are three . . ." from *Bama, Bear Bryant and the Bible: 100 Devotionals Based on the Life of Paul* by David Shepard, iUniverse, 2002, page 3.

"Pain can break us or make us . . ." from *Resilience: Hard-Won Wisdom for Living a Better Life* by Eric Greitens, Houghton Mifflin Harcourt, 2015, page 4.

"But it ain't about how hard you hit . . ." from *Rocky Balboa*, 2006.

Chapter 16

"We can create a psychological . . ." from "Sorrow And Hope," *Sports Illustrated*, May 23, 2011, and available at http://www.si.com/vault/2012/01/19/106151261/sorrow-and-hope

"hugged more people than anyone ever has . . ." from "April 27 tornado 'softened' Nick Saban, ensured 'he would never leave,' author Lars Anderson says," *Al.com*, August 18, 2014, and available at http://www.al.com/sports/index.ssf/2014/08/tuscaloosa_tornado_softened_ni.html

Chapter 17

"There are two paths people can take . . ." from *Falling Forward* by John C. Maxwell, Harper Collins, 2007.

"I know of no other way to triumph . . ." from *Desiring God: Meditations of a Christian Hedonist* by John Piper, Crown Publishing Group, 2011, page 13.

Chapter 18

"Christ never intended . . ." available at http://www.azquotes.com/quote/1191381

"The great spiritual call of the Beloved . . ." from *Life of the Beloved: Spiritual Living in a Secular World* by Henri J.M. Nouwen, The Crossroad Publishing Company, 2002.

Chapter 19

"I run on the road . . ." Muhammad Ali, quoted in *Strength of a Cham-*

pion: Finding Faith and Fortitude Through Adversity by O.J. Brigance and Peter Schrager, Penguin, 2013.

"This is the great challenge for us today . . ." from *Chasing Elephants* by Brent Crowe, NavPress, 2010.

Chapter 20

"Our greatest fear should . . ." quoted in *Live Your Calling: A Practical Guide to Finding and Fulfilling Your Mission in Life* by Kevin Brennfleck and Kay Marie Brennfleck, John Wiley & Sons, 2004, page 197.

Chapter 21

"So the Tide showed us . . ." from "President Obama Welcomes BCS Champion University of Alabama Crimson Tide," *WhiteHouse.gov,* April 19, 2012, and available at https://www.whitehouse.gov/photos-and-video/video/2012/04/19/president-obama-welcomes-bcs-champion-university-alabama-crimson-t

Chapter 22

"It is not what we get but who . . ." Tony Robbins, quoted in *$500,000* *Worth of Inspiring Quotations of our Times* by Web Augustine, Lulu. com, 2011, page 152.

"Only those who have learned . . ." Tony Robbins, quoted in *Unleash Your Inner Warrior: How to Change Your Mindset for the Better, Soar with the Eagles, and Live the Life of Your Dreams* by Brad C. Wenneberg, Morgan James Publishing, 2009.

Chapter 23

"You see the giant and the shepherd in the Valley . . ." from *David and Goliath: Underdogs, Misfits, and the Art of Battling Giants* by Malcolm Gladwell, Little, Brown, 2013.

"If you have a beautiful story . . ." from "Q&A with Author Donald

Miller," *Relevant*, November 20, 2009, and available at http://www.relevantmagazine.com/culture/books/features/19094-qaa-with-donald-miller

Chapter 25

"The ultimate measure of a man . . ." from *Strength to Love* by Martin Luther King, Fortress Press, 1977, page 35.

Chapter 26

"When something happens to you . . ." from *A Million Miles in a Thousand Years: What I Learned While Editing My Life* by Donald Miller, Thomas Nelson Inc., 2009.

"Don't give up. Don't ever give up . . ." from *Don't Give Up...Don't Ever Give Up: The Inspiration of Jimmy V.* by Justin Spizman and Robyn Spizman, Sourcebooks, Inc., 2010.

Chapter 28

"Without your wound . . ." from *Abba's Child: The Cry of the Heart for Intimate Belonging* by Brennan Manning, NavPress, 2015, page 12.

"If we're growing we're . . ." John Maxwell, quoted in *Everything is Personal: Changing the Beliefs That Block Our Inner Happiness and Peace of Mind* by Connie Beyer, LifeRich Publishing, 2015.

Chapter 29

"Life is a gift, and it offers . . ." from *Awaken the Giant Within* by Tony Robbins, Simon and Schuster, 2012.

"When you die, it does not mean that you . . ." from "Stuart Scott's ESPYs speech was his finest television moment," *USA Today*, July 17, 2014, and available at http://ftw.usatoday.com/2014/07/stuart-scott-espys-speech-espn-valvano-cancer.

Chapter 30

"Don't ever discount the wonder . . ." from *The Shack* by William P. Young, Windblown Media, 2008.

ACKNOWLEDGMENTS

Pain is a reality of life. Eventually, everyone goes through some sort of pain. I have experienced pain. I have won, and I have lost. The amazing thing for me though is that when I experienced hardship, I did not go through it alone. I had a loving family by my side the entire time. I am forever grateful for everyone that played a part in helping me fight through the pain.

My family was my greatest strength in the depths of the pain I experienced. My beautiful mother, my strong father, my late brother Trent, and my goofy brother T.J. are my strength and my motivation today. My wonderful Nana, who has a heart of gold, taught me each and every day to give, because it's not about *getting* a blessing—it's about *being* a blessing.

I am very thankful for the Core Media Group, Stephen and Robert, for helping me get my story of moving through pain toward triumph to print. Even before the Core Media Group, I was blessed to have Susan and Emily help me get this book started. For that, I could never repay you, but I am forever grateful.

Coach Saban and Coach Cochran, you helped me become the man I am today while coaching me at the University of Alabama. Your willingness to each write a foreword in support of this book speaks volumes of your character and your genuine love for your players and former players.

To the Karn family, I am so blessed that God brought us together. Little did I know after meeting Linlee in 2010 that your family would become my own. I know that you guys are going through a storm right now after losing Linlee's brother, David Gilchrist Karn, on September 1, 2015, right before this book went to print. I am sorry for your loss. It's okay to not be okay. Over the years, Gilchrist became the older brother I never had, and I know he is dancing in heaven with Trent right now. Through tragedy and despair, I have personally seen the hope and joy that only comes from God. He can and *will* grant that to you. It is because of situations like this that this book even exists: to give hope to the masses.

To the Bibb County community, this book is for you. To the University of Alabama, this book is for you. To my high school and college coaches, this book is for you. To my teammates at Bibb County and at Alabama, this book is for you. To all my family and friends, this book is for you. To anyone who has experienced pain, this book is for you. Although this may be perceived as my story, this is also your story.

There wouldn't be a single page of this book without the thousands of people who have invested in me over the years. Coaches, teachers, friends, and family have all played a major role in this happening. Thank you for the sacrifice you all have made.

Someone in particular believed in me, invested in this book, and told me, "This story is not just yours, Taylor—it's all of ours. That's why I am investing." That person was my elementary school principal Ms. Carol Belcher.

Thank you all for being a blessing.